ALLAN MORRISON was a daily passenger on the number 9 Auchenshuggle tram for over three years. He, like many other Glaswegians, still laments the passing of Glasgow's wonderful tram network. *Last Tram tae Auchenshuggle!* combines three of his passions: humour, nostalgia and Glasgow.

Allan is the author of 16 books. His media appearances include The One Show, Richard and Judy and The Fred McAulay Show.

He is involved in charity work, after-dinner speaking and is a member of his local Rotary club. Allan enjoys hill-walking, sport and travel. He and his wife live in the West of Scotland and he is the proud grandfather of four grandchildren.

Last Tram tae Auchenshuggle!

Have a final shoogle with
Glasgow's famous conductress,
big Aggie MacDonald

ALLAN MORRISON

Illustrated by
Mitch Miller

Luath Press Limited
EDINBURGH
www.luath.co.uk

First published 2011

ISBN : 978-1-908373-04-5

Printed and bound by
Martins the Printers, Berwick Upon Tweed

Typeset in 11 point Sabon
by 3btype.com

Glasgow Corporation Tramway System, Schematic Diagram
by Ron Sheridan

Contents

Acknowledgements

My grateful thanks go to the following people: Brian Longworth of the Scottish Tramway and Transport Society, Val Grieve, Anne McGregor, Andrew Pearson, Lynne Roper, Ron and Anne Sheridan, Archie Wilson, John and Morag Wilson.

Introduction

Nostalgia and humour are a potent mix. Reminisce, laugh or cry, at an era in Glasgow of trams, tracks and tenements as Big Aggie MacDonald, the famous tramcar conductress, rides the Glasgow 'caurs' (as the trams were referred to by Glaswegians) during their final years, before taking the *Last Tram tae Auchenshuggle* in September 1962.

The auld shoogly tram was a microcosm of Glasgow. All social groups used the caurs: the elderly; young folks; parents with children; shoppers laden with purchases; shipyard workers in bunnets and overalls; city gents in bowler hats (they would only travel in the lower deck saloon, of course!); and tourists. In fact, everyone going about their daily business. Trams were the life blood of Glasgow as they clanged, shoogled, swayed, shuddered, lurched and screeched throughout the city.

For Glaswegians, travelling on rails provided a friendly intimacy and sense of security. Passengers sat chatting, reading their newspapers, or listening to the cheeky Glasgow patois of the conductress or conductor. Often the caurs were full with people left holding on to straps, cheek-by-jowl, while moaning about the overcrowding, the weather or the football.

To this day the caurs remain *the* focus of nostalgic folk history in Glasgow. It is a love affair which seems to grow with the passage of time as they evoke wonderful memories for many people.

Last Tram tae Auchenshuggle is a trip down memory lane to 1962 when the Glasgow tram service is shortly to end. But Aggie is not finished yet. She wants to enjoy the last months on her beloved caurs, dishing out advice and patter with her razor sharp wit to the unwary: the outspoken clippie who was never outspoken!

Major Events of 1962

10 February	American spy pilot Gary Powers is exchanged for a Soviet spy.
4 April	James Hanratty is hanged in Bedford for the A6 murder.
9 April	*West Side Story* wins the Oscar for Best Picture.
14 April	Scotland beats England 2–0 at Hampden.
24 May	Scott Carpenter orbits the earth three times in the *Aurora* 7 space capsule.
26 May	Acker Bilk's 'Stranger on the Shore' achieves number one in the US charts.
17 June	Brazil wins the World Cup in Chile, beating Czechoslovakia 3–1 in the final.
10 July	Telstar, the world's first commercial communications satellite, is launched.
5 August	Actress, Marilyn Monroe, dies.
4 September	End of the Glasgow Tramway System. The last tram goes to Auchenshuggle.
25 September	Sonny Liston beats Floyd Patterson to win the World Heavyweight Boxing Title.
5 October	First James Bond film, *Dr No*, starring Scot, Sean Connery, premieres in the UK.

14 October   Cuban Missile Crisis begins.

22 December   The Big Freeze starts in Scotland;
                 it was to last until 5 March 1963.

The Magic of Auchenshuggle

Auchenshuggle! Just saying the name is pure joy. It's one of those satisfying evocative words you can really get your teeth into. It could easily be used as a mild swear word, so vehement is the emphasis placed on those four syllables. Indeed it is so catchy that Auchenshuggle was adapted by the *Sunday Post* to become Auchenshoogle, the home town of *Oor Wullie*.

So where does this quintessentially Scottish name come from? *Achadh an t- Seagail* in Scottish Gaelic means 'field of rye'. 'Shuggle' is to sway, rock or be rickety. A field of swaying crops is a description which could easily have been applied to a convoy of Glasgow trams as it oscillated from side to side.

Many people thought that Glasgow Corporation Transport Department had 'done a Hollywood' with their General Manager of the time, James Dalrymple, deliberately inventing this wonderful place name Auchenshuggle to emblazon on the front of the trams as a gimmick, in order to encourage curious people to travel there to increase revenue.

In the 19th century Auchenshuggle was a small group of cottages set east of Glasgow. It came to prominence when in 1922 the eastern terminus of the number 9 (red) tram was changed from Springfield Road to Auchenshuggle. There was no regular service beyond Auchenshuggle and the terminus was situated at the City Boundary where London Road widened just beyond four old villas on the east side of Braidfauld Street, now occupied by flats. Part of the service was extended to Carmyle in 1944 but was cut back again in 1952, then the terminus was moved further east towards Causewayside Street.

The number 9 tram ran from Dalmuir West Terminus in Dumbarton Road, Dalmuir, at the junction with Mountblow Road, going through Clydebank, Yoker, Scotstoun, Partick and the centre of Glasgow, ending up east of Braidfauld Street in Auchenshuggle. At this point was the crossover junction from the outbound line to the inbound line. When the trams were replaced, a bus-only turning circle was created at the west corner of London Road and Braidfauld Street.

The famous number 9 originated as a 'red' service along Argyle Street together with numbers 26 and 26A. This busy route ran through tenement housing and industrial areas which meant traffic was heavy. Indeed it was almost impossible not to see a tramcar when one looked along the length of Argyle Street.

In 1962 there was an impending sense of profound loss as Glaswegians steeled themselves, not only to lose their beloved caurs, but also to lose what was really a way of life. There was something of a 'wind of change' blowing through Britain at that time, and many radical alterations were being made in the name of modernisation and progress.

The last official trams ran in Glasgow on Saturday the 1 September 1962.

However it was felt that some special trams should run for a few days more and as a result a very limited service was operated between Anderston Cross and Auchenshuggle, the last tram for paying passengers leaving at five o'clock on the evening of 4 September to Auchenshuggle. This marked the end of a remarkable era of unique public transport.

On that evening, a final commemorative parade of 20 trams led by a horse-drawn caur from 1894 attracted an estimated quarter of a million Glaswegians who had shown their unashamed affection by clinging to their trams to the very last. They had turned out to say goodbye to this endearing part of city life, as the trams shoogled into scrapyards, museums (as far away as America) and history books.

Last tram tae Auchenshuggle,
Last tram tae Auchenshuggle.
If you miss this one,
You'll never get another one,
The number 9, to Auchenshuggle.

The trams may have gone but the name of Auchenshuggle has been given a new lease of life with the Auchenshuggle Bridge (opened 2011) which now carries both carriageways of the M74 across the River Clyde. The area has been further invigorated with a business park located next to Auchenshuggle Woods, south of London Road.

'I Remember the Trams'

'What do I remember o' the trams? Everything: the cheek o' the conductresses; the big brass handle that the driver used; the smell of chips and fish suppers; the blue and sometimes red sparks on the overhead wires at night; the ping of the clippie's ticket machine. Also, the ritual at the terminus when the destination blind was changed, usually with a loud clatter, and the bow collector was reversed for the return journey. I can see it all as if it was yesterday. Good days, they were.'

GRAEME M

❖ ❖

'I can recall the last days of the tramcars. We lived near Anderston Cross and I thought I would take my two wee boys for a last trip on the caurs. We managed to get upstairs all the way to Auchenshuggle. It wis sad, but the boys fair enjoyed the experience, waving out the windows at the crowds.'

ELEANOR S

❖ ❖

'What I recall most vividly was the racket, because they were noisy beasts. Aye, I can still hear the bogies chaffing as they went round a junction, hitting the rail-joints. The bow collector on the overhead wires gave a kinda swish, but the best bit was if you got a conductress *who gave it laldy wi' the patter. It was better than going to the Empire! Some of their cheeky remarks were legend.'*

HECTOR M

❖ ❖

'Ah remember the trams late at night when it was dark. They moved around like a ship, all lit up with flying sparks off the bow collector when they hit a junction. Inside they wad rattle like an auld tin can filled with nails.'

AGNES P

❖ ❖

'It was awfa sad. Everybuddy was near greetin'. We stood watching the tram procession. You see, we'd been brought up wi' the trams. They were a way of life in Glesca.'

PETER M

❖ ❖

'What sticks in my mind is when I was a wee boy going on a tram from Springburn to Linthouse. There was a melodious drunk who serenaded us wi' a' the Scots songs. Then he gave us 'I Belang Tae Glasgow', and the whole lower deck, including the conductress, joined in. Magic!'

ANDREW B

❖ ❖

'Our family lived in Renfrew and we would visit an old relation of my mother's who lived just outside Milngavie. The journey seemed to take quite a while, and it was

not until many years later that I discovered it was 22 miles, the longest route on the Glasgow Transport Tram System, as well as being the longest in Britain.'

JIM M

❖ ❖

'Saturday was our big day on the trams. We took the caur tae Rouken Glen, if the weather was good. The problem was that everybody seemed to have the same idea. The caurs were overflowing and so was the park. But it was great fun, both on the journey there, and at the boating pond at the park.'

MARGARET S

❖ ❖

'I used to go into the City Centre with my pal, Frank. We would jump on a tram at a junction, hold on to the platform-handle, and get a free ride. Then the conductress would see us and if you didn't jump off you could get a thick ear, and she would shout, "Ur youse jist actin' daft tae get a free hurl?" They wouldn't allow anybody to do that nowadays, but that was the way it was in the '50s. Anyway it didn't deter us. We would just hop on another caur till we were caught again. Many a time we got into town without having to pay anything.'

BRIAN T

❖ ❖

'On the Sabbath I had to dress up in my 'Sunday Best'
along with my wee sister, and go on a number 26 tram
to Burnside to see my 'posh' granny. She was my maternal
granny, and lived in this large house with a garden.
Different from the back green at our tenement I can
tell you.'

DIANE L

❖ ❖

'You could say that the trams were synonymous with
Glasgow. They were like the character of the city, you
know, hardy and dependable. You took them for granted
– then suddenly they were gone. The buses and trolley-
buses were bland with no character whatsoever. I am
sure they could have modernised the tram fleet. The early
'60s was not the time to change the transport system
as Glasgow's industries were forging ahead. It was a
crying shame.'

ALEX M

❖ ❖

'The humour can be great at a football match if you
stand beside a couple of wags. But let me tell you, it is
nothing compared to the 'Glesca patois' you could get
on a tram. If you came across certain conductresses
then the entertainment would be rich. If the patter to
and fro was sparklin', then you were reluctant to get
off at your stop.'

WILLIAM R

'Just before the Second World War I was walking down Sauchiehall Street holding my father's hand. Suddenly sirens went off, but it wasn't an air raid, it was 11 o'clock on 11 November. A tram stopped beside us, and the motorman and the conductor got out. They took their hats off and stood beside the tram. Quite a few passengers joined them. Then the sirens went off again and they all got back into the caur and away it went.'

WILLIAM M

❖ ❖

'See when I go on the number 64 bus from Carmyle to the City Centre, and it stops in Braidfauld Street, Auchenshuggle, I can still see, and smell, the old number 9 tram. Good days they were back then.'

SADIE S

❖ ❖

'My father always said the trams looked like sardine tins on their side with all the sardines looking out. Sometimes it felt like that when the whole tram inside was choc-a-bloc. The only difference was that sardines don't talk and by golly Glaswegians can blether better than anybody. You could make friendships or find romance on the tram. For a time I even went out with a lass I stood beside on a tram which was filled to the gunnels with folk. I can even remember an old poem about love on a Glasgow tramcar.'

PETER M

'Twas sweet of old,
As our love we told,
On the top o' an auld Glesca caur.
When a wandering breeze
Made us cough and sneeze,
Wi' the smell o' fags and cigars.

When the lights were low,
And the caur was aglow,
And many a miss got a kiss.
Wi' a cuddle an' squeeze,
I got doon on my knees,
And a wee lassie became 'a wife'.

ANON

'I remember the trams in smog when they rang a warning bell for all and sundry. At least you felt safe in a tram in those conditions. The problems started when you had to get off and you could hardly see your hand in front of your face. If you didn't have the fare home in a pea-souper then everyone just followed the tramlines. And another thing, I always fancied being a conductress and flicking over the seats at the terminus. They were like a pack of cards or dominoes.'

DOROTHY C

❖ ❖

'From my auntie's window you could hear the hiss on the overhead wires plus the 'thump-click' as the wheels crossed the nearby junction.'

ELEANOR C

❖ ❖

'With very little opposition in the way of cars, the trams were 'kings of the road' in the '30s and '40s. As a result they could fairly clank along unhindered by the kind of volume of traffic we have nowadays.'

BILL T

❖ ❖

'A friend of mine is a tram enthusiast. He says that watching a line of trams coming towards you was like seeing an armada of warships sailing off to battle. I agree with him for they certainly were impressive in their hey day.'

THOMAS D

'My favourite trams were the ones that went down Parliamentary Road. They could get up to a fantastic speed. It was better than the Big Dipper in Blackpool. Some of these trams flew along like the hammers o' hell!'

MATT L

❖ ❖

'I used to love to ride on a tram. My mother gave me a jammy piece wrapped in wax paper off a loaf, and my pals and I would sit there wobbling along in the wee cabin directly above the driver. There was a sliding door separating us from the rest of the passengers on the top deck. We could make a bit of a noise unless we stamped our feet. Then the motorman (driver) would use rich language telling us to stop the racket. We were able to go to a terminus, right across the city, where we'd never been before, and then come safely home, all for a penny.'

ROBERT F

❖ ❖

'It's the reverberations off the tenements that I recall. I can still hear them today. It was sort of like a train going through a canyon. Funnily enough you became used to it. When the caurs finished Glasgow became quieter. I just loved they old caurs.'

JENNIFER P

❖ ❖

'We had an old wireless. When the trams passed our close sometimes you got a bit of interference. It was annoying if you were listening to the 'Top-Twenty' on Radio Luxembourg.'

SANDY G

❖ ❖

'We used to put old pennies on the tramline then watch as the tram ran over them. It was kinda stupid as the coin was then bent or flattened and useless so you couldn't use it. A've still got one in a drawer somewhere at home. A sort of souvenir. What I also remember was one of my pals mistakenly putting down a half-crown instead of a penny. Boy was he upset!'

GERALD M

❖ ❖

Big Aggie MacDonald

Ferrs pal-eeze, ferrs pal-eeze,
Ye a' can hear me sing,
As up an' doon the sterrs ah go
An' gie ma bell a ring.
Ah work fur the Corporation-
Ye'll tell it by ma dress-
Ah'm Aggie MacDonald fae Gorbals Cross;
The caur conductress.

Glasgow had many weel-kent tram conductresses, but Big Aggie MacDonald, the original 'big-yin', was the doyenne of them all. A dominating, ebullient, self-assured extrovert, it was generally agreed that she was 'something else' when it came to dealing with fare dodgers ('pauchlers'), drunks, nyaffs, recalcitrant weans, and pretentious, high falutin' passengers with 'pan loaf' accents who came from the posher areas of the city or lived in half-tiled wally closes. Aggie relished pricking the pomposity of the hoity-toity with her belligerent use of the Glasgow vernacular infused with her own brand of dark humour. Aggie demanded respect as she shouted with her strong, rich voice, smoke cured by decades of cigarettes, 'Right, aw youse! Nae staunin' up top. Move right doon the caur! Haud tight ontae yer strap or yer man.' Then she would ring the bell, and the tram would lurch into life, rolling along like the proverbial Glasgow drunk.

Aggie was called 'big' because that best described her many dimensions. No longer in the flower of her

FORAGE CAP

BOTTLE BLONDE HAIR

BADGE

UNIFORM (BOTTLE GREEN)

WELL-UPHOLSTERED

IMPOSING

TICKET MACHINE

MASSIVE HANDS

MONEY BAG

HIGH RUMPED

FEET - CAN KICK A SIX-FOOTER UP TO SIX FEET

youth, she was tall, imposing, high-rumped and well-upholstered, just like her beloved trams. Her eyes could on occasions be kindly, but at first glance passengers correctly came to the conclusion that here was a formidable woman. Aggie's hair was determinedly bottle-blonde, but with grey creeping in at the edges. Going upstairs to collect fares was no longer a quick jaunt for Aggie due to her weight and ongoing lungfuls of smoke. On many occasions fares were collected with a cigarette, mostly composed of ash, hanging out of the corner of a red-lipsticked mouth, while she came out with loud, blinding put-downs or wisecracks. Aggie had massive hands to match her body and personality, and despite thick, nicotine stained fingers, her dexterity in handling change was impressive. The exception to Aggie's occasional tirades was when the passenger was a good-looking man, for our heroine had a liking for the opposite sex.

With Aggie's needle-sharp perceptiveness, any person trying to jouk a ride on her tram was in for a rude awakening, much to the amusement of the other passengers. Aggie would say, 'Everybuddy is entitled tae ma opinion!' and she certainly dished it out. Needless to say Aggie was forever fighting with 'The Hats' and 'The Gestapo', as inspectors were called. But our no-nonsense heroine usually won.

Travelling by tram could be most entertaining, especially listening to a domineering matriarch like Big Aggie, with her caustic humour and cheeky patter all delivered in a gallus, rasping voice.

Yes, riding on Aggie's tram was pure theatre.

The Conductresses

During world war 1, with over 3,000 tram crew at the front in France (one in six never came back), the Corporation started to recruit women as motormen (drivers) and conductresses. By 1951, 40 per cent of tram crews were women. Women were to play a major part in the tramway system right to the end in September 1962. Tram conductresses and conductors spent three days at the Corporation's Training School in Govan. Instructions were given on the handling of money, the use of the ticket machine, ensuring passengers were dealt with in accordance with regulations, and the use of the bell. A single bell told the driver to stop; two bells to go; three bells meant 'stop at once as I require your assistance'; four bells indicated that the tram was full and the driver should continue beyond the next stop. Any passenger who had the audacity to ring the bell to disembark would immediately incur the wrath of many a conductress or conductor who regarded that as their sole responsibility.

No more than ten people were allowed to stand on the lower deck although this rule did not apply to the last tram at night. Standing passengers mostly used the ceiling handrails or the leather straps attached to them.

No one could stand on the upper-deck. However Big Aggie MacDonald and her likes sometimes made up their own rules to suit each situation. On one occasion a tram inspector discovered 55 passengers standing throughout a tramcar.

The uniform was bottle green, heavy-serge material with red piping. It was normally worn regardless of the season. Conductors wore peaked caps. Conductresses were not allowed to wear headscarves and their headwear was a beret until 1956 when a forage cap, based on the design of an air hostess' headwear, was introduced. A high standard was demanded, and if you were not properly dressed, and if your buttons and badge were unpolished, you would not be allowed on your shift and therefore perhaps lose wages with a suspension. Most employees, however, wore their uniform with pride.

New employees were allocated to a specific depot. After two or three days out with an experienced conductress or conductor they were then on their own.

Being a conductress was hard going. They could find themselves standing for up to eight hours while weighed down by a heavy ticket-issuing machine and a cash bag of copper half-pennies and pennies, forever increasing in weight. Many conductresses and conductors encouraged passengers to change their three-penny bits, sixpences, shillings, florins or half-crowns into coppers (they were useful at home for the gas meter), thereby relieving them on an on-going basis of some of the weight around their necks. However there was always the conductor's ticket machine box below the stairs, preferably at the end where the driver was, into which excess coinage could be deposited.

Tram shifts could start as early as 4am with the final shifts finishing at 1am. Split-shifts were common, and as most depots were located in tenement districts, it was useful if you lived close to your depot in order that some rest could be had during the break.

The pay was not wonderful either: it peaked around the £11 per week mark when the trams finally finished in 1962.

Fares were relatively cheap: from 1956 it was tuppence ha'penny for two stages, four pence for three or four stages, and sixpence for longer journeys. Tram fares were cheaper than bus fares up until they were synchronised in 1959. It is also interesting that it was most unusual for anyone to tender even a ten shilling (50 pence) note for a ticket.

Many people still have unique and irreplaceable recollections of the Glasgow tram conductresses, their work ethic and their patter.

The Shouts of the Glasgow Tram Conductresses

'If this is yer stop, get aff.
If no, stay on an' gie us yer chaff!'

❖ ❖

'Ma caur's full! Ah said nae mair!
No' even up the sterr. Ur youse aw deef?'

❖ ❖

'If them that's cummin' oan'll get aff,
them that's getting' aff'll get oan better.'

❖ ❖

'Right aw youse. Nae staunin' up tap.
There's seats doon the sterr.'

❖ ❖

'Here we are fur where we're goin'.
Aw them that's here fur there, get aff!'

❖ ❖

'Get aff! O-f-f, aff! Dae ye no'
understaun' the Queen's English?'

❖ ❖

'Right! Move further doon the caur!
Ferrs, pal-leeze!'

❖ ❖

'If yer gaun, then cummoan,
if yer no' then get aff!'

❖ ❖

'This caur's no' movin' wan inch
till everywan o' youse is aff this platform!'

❖ ❖

'Hurry up. Cummoanangetaff!
We huvnae goat aw day.'

❖ ❖

'Wur full! Everybuddy haud ontae
a strap or yer man!'

❖ ❖

The Glasgow Caurs

Oh, ye cannae get tae Heaven oan a Standard Glesca
*   tram,*
Fur a Glesca tram it disnae go that far.'
Wi' a prayer ye might make it to Drumchapel or
*   Clydebank,*
If ye keep on riding past the Trongate Bar.
Ma faither says that ye can take the caur tae Timbuktu,
(But me, ah don't believe a single word.)
No, ye cannae go tae Heaven on yer Standard Glesca
*   tram,*
Fur even a Glesca tram cannae go that far.

ANON

The tramcar was a faithful servant to the Glasgow
public for over 90 years. It was also a major
employer of labour with at one time ten thousand
employees being involved in the tramway system.
Over the years the trams became an integral way of life
in Glasgow providing excellent, affordable travel
throughout the sprawling metropolis. There was an
abundance of convenient stops throughout the city and
trams ran from early morning to very late at night. In
addition to the caur stops a number of 'loading islands',
in the middle of a road, were erected. The noise of

trams as they clattered over the intricate web of rails at complex junctions, or swerved sharply around tight bends, became the normal sounds of Glasgow life.

The gauge between the rails was four feet, seven and three quarter inches (1.416m). This was to permit standard gauge railway wagons to operate over sections of the tram system, especially those close to the Clyde shipyards and railway freight yards. The Vale of Clyde track between Fairfield's Shipyard and Govan Cross had originally been laid as a goods track to link the shipyard with the national railway lines. This meant that the trams could run on the rail top, and the railway wagons and trains on their flanges in the groove of the embedded rail. The entire tramway network was laid at the same gauge, which was fine until the Corporation bought second-hand trams from Liverpool, when some re-gauging had to be carried out.

It is of further interest to note that all tramways departments were responsible for maintaining the granite setts between the rails, and for 18 inches either side of them.

The trams came into being in Glasgow on 19 August 1872, when the St George's Cross to Eglinton Toll tram line was established, a distance of two and a quarter miles. They were horse-drawn and could seat up to 40 passengers. A few had tartan livery. Some of the trams had coil springs, others leaf-type springs. Both provided passengers with a bumpy ride. Unfortunately the trams were heavy and cumbersome, and horses were continually injuring themselves on the street cobbles, especially in winter. If a horse fell over then the passengers would watch as the driver sat by the horse's head, talking to the animal to calm it down while the conductor unhitched the beast from the tram. Usually a hood would be put over its head until it stood up.

Eventually over 3,000 horses in nine depots were required to operate the 31 miles of network. The speed was anything up to ten miles per hour. Collecting manure in buckets for gardens was a by-product of the early tramway system.

A story of the time explains how a Glasgow drunk watched as a tram driver was trying to put the hood on a rather fractious horse. Eventually the drunk could stand it no longer and blurted out:

'Ye'll never do it, ye know. Ye'll never do it.'

'Never do what?' asked the driver.

'Ye'll never pit that big hoarse in that wee bag.'

Steam-powered trams were run in the south of the city by the Vale of Clyde Tramways Company. The fare was a penny to sit inside or a half-penny on the open top deck. It was not unusual on an inclement day to observe all of the passengers on top sitting with open umbrellas, and, if it was very wet, straw was spread on the floor.

The electrification of the tram system began in 1898. 'Room and Kitchen' or 'But and Ben' cars were Glasgow's first electric trams. In total 21 were built. They were single deck vehicles with a central door. Glaswegians called them 'room and kitchen' caurs because they, like some tenement flats, were divided into two sections. Some were also referred to as 'sparkies', presumably referring to the sparks from the trolleys and wheels. They ran from 1898 until 1906. One was eventually converted into a mains testing car and is now in the Riverside Museum in Glasgow back in its original condition.

By 1902, over 500 electric tramcars were in service. As a result the city-wide horse-drawn service was withdrawn by the end of that year. The new trams were initially fitted with trolley poles to take the electricity from the overhead wire, but they were later replaced with bow collectors. At that time the tramway network also generated its own cost efficient electricity at Pinkston Power Station in Port Dundas. Eventually all of the city's trams, trolley-buses and underground system were powered from Pinkston. Pinkston was finally closed down in 1976.

The Standard Tram was the mainstay of the Glasgow fleet. They were four-wheeled, double-deck vehicles weighing in excess of 12 tons. A heavy bogie was necessary especially in case the caur became a 'swinger', ie full of passengers.

The first versions had rounded front panels and open tops (later closed in). They had bare light bulbs; also distinctive moquette seats. Over a thousand Standards were built between 1898 and 1924, operating on all of the 200 plus miles of tramlines in Glasgow. They could seat 21 passengers on the lower deck with 38 on the top deck. It did not take long before

Glaswegians became used to the multifarious noises of their brakes, valves and compressors. The old Standards were used almost until the closure of the tramway system as they were able to navigate difficult clearances such as Parkhead Cross that the more modern vehicles could not work on. Standards were referred to by Glaswegians as the 'Auld Caurs' as distinct from later models.

The 'Kilmarnock' tram was introduced in 1927 and was a variation of the Standard tram, but had eight wheels (two four-wheeled bogies). The crews called them 'Double-Bogies'. These trams were constructed by four different manufacturers to a common design, but all the bogies themselves were made by the Kilmarnock Engineering Company, hence their name. Unfortunately there were problems with derailing on points. They could not clatter over the junctions like the old Standards. 'Kilmarnocks' were restricted to comparatively straight routes such as Dalmuir West to Auchenshuggle.

By the 1930s it was recognised that the Glasgow tram fleet was becoming dated. Other British cities had taken decisions to modernise their tramway system (a few actually abandoning them at this time). With the pending Empire Exhibition at Bellahouston Park in 1938 it was decided that extra trams would be required to transport the expected volume of visitors. A new fleet of 150 double-deck trams eventually came on stream, all built at the Coplawhill Works. They had cosy saloons and much improved lighting. Also one of their advantages was that there was no requirement to hang out the top deck's window to change the destination screen, as these screens were now contained in a cabinet within the tram.

The first was delivered in 1937, the year of the Coronation of King George VI, and eventually were called 'Coronations'. Coronation number 1142 had a special Royal livery of red, silver-grey and blue, distinct from the normal green, cream and orange. It was used at the Empire Exhibition in 1938, attended by the King and Queen.

The 'Cunarder' trams were a post-war development of the Coronation trams and were introduced in 1948. They were similar to the Coronation trams, but with small differences such as the route indicator being above the side window of the cab rather than the front of the tram, the idea being it was easier for potential passengers to identify their intended caur in a line of approaching trams. Also they didn't have the etched glass mirrored decoration of the Coronation. Unfortunately they had three steps from street level which made them less popular with the older generation. A hundred were built at Glasgow Corporation Transport's Coplawhill Works.

When it was decided to close Liverpool's tram system in 1954, 46 of their streamlined trams were purchased by Glasgow Corporation. The cost was five hundred pounds each. They were two feet longer than the Coronation trams but because of clearance problems they were confined to two routes which had only a few tight curves (Broomhouse to Milngavie, and Baillieston to Anderston Cross). Conductresses, like Big Aggie, disliked these caurs, behemoths named 'Green Goddesses', as they seated 78 passengers, 14 more than the other tram models. Over time they were gradually withdrawn, the final one finishing in 1960.

Adhering to the timetable was fundamental. Drivers had to clock-in at 'Bundy clocks', strategically placed throughout in the city. These were policed by the many tram inspectors who were forever jumping on and off trams inspecting passengers' tickets.

In the early years of World War II many trams were fitted with anti-blast netting: also fenders were painted white during the blackout period. Unfortunately some were victims of Goering's Luftwaffe bombers. A caur was destroyed in Nelson Street in the Gorbals, and a number of trams reduced to shells during the Clydebank Blitz. However trams played a significant part in the war years, especially during the blackout when the tram's dependability allowed the transportation of passengers to continue. During air raid warnings, trams would slow to a crawl. The official term for this was 'a purple warning'. Only if a raid was imminent did service personnel and other passengers leave the tram to take shelter.

Due to petrol rationing during the war, private motoring was limited which meant many more people took to the trams. Ration books were issued to motorists providing sufficient petrol to travel 200 miles a month. The amount of petrol a motorist received varied according to engine size. Some people added paraffin to their petrol which was surprisingly efficient but made engines noisy. Passengers alighting from trams could be hit by the smell of paraffin from passing traffic on the road. Petrol rationing did not finish until May 1950.

There is an interesting statistic from those war years. In 1944 there were over 1,200 trams, the fare takings totalling £3,173,865 for the year.

Tram routes were not given numbers until 1938. Prior to that colour-coded bands denoted various routes, the colours of the trams were denoted by the colour band round the top section of the vehicle, as in the early years of the trams many people in the city allegedly could not read. People were deemed to be poor or rich depending on which tram route they lived for example, if you were on a yellow route then you were perceived as well-off.

RED

8   Bishopbriggs / Springburn / Millerston / Riddrie / Alexandra Park / Newlands / Giffnock / Rouken Glen.

9   Dalmuir West / Auchenshuggle.

9a   Scotstoun / Burnside.

9b   Scotstoun / Rutherglen.

11   Maryhill / Gairbraid Avenue / Sinclair Drive.

13   Mount Florida / Hillfoot / Milngavie.

17   Cambuslang / Anniesland.

BLUE

4   Keppochhill Road / Renfrew / Porterfield Road.

4a   Springburn / Linthouse.

4b   Lambhill / Linthouse.

6   Riddrie / Alexandra Park / Scotstoun / Dalmuir West.

10   Rutherglen / Kirklee.

14   Milngavie / Hillfoot / Maryhill / Renfrew Ferry.

WHITE

2   Provanmill / Polmadie.

3   University / Mosspark / Eglinton Street.

3a   University / Mosspark / Paisley Road West.

18   Springburn / Rutherglen / Burnside.

19   Springburn / Netherlee.

GREEN

1   Knightswood / Kelvinside / Airdrie.

1a   Dalmuir West / Scotstounhill / Springfield Road.

15   Airdrie / Paisley / Ferguslie Mills.

15a   Uddingston / Tollcross / Paisley / Ferguslie Mills.

16   Whiteinch / Keppochhill Road.

YELLOW

5   Clarkston / Kirklee.

5a   Langside / Jordanhill.

7   Millerston / Riddrie / Craigton Road.

12   Mount Florida / Paisley Road Toll.

NO COLOUR

20   Yoker / Clydebank / Duntocher.

During the war years the colour code system was
gradually being phased out and by 1952 had
completely gone. After 1949, route numbers mostly
went from 1 to 40 with a few exceptions. Subsequently
services were gradually withdrawn and replaced or
merged with bus or trolley-bus services. The first to go
was in 1949, when the number 2 from Provanmill to
Polmadie was changed to a trolleybus service.

   In certain winter conditions smoke from countless
homes and industrial chimneys combined to produce
smog, a soot-laden blanket of thick fog usually referred
to as a 'pea-souper'. Buses and cars were almost useless

in such conditions. Many a motorist would follow a tram only to find themselves inside a tram depot shed. Although the tram would crawl through the City in such conditions it was still able to get passengers to their destination, albeit slowly. A warning bell (the 'gong') would be used by the driver to let other traffic and waiting passengers know that a tram was coming. Many other people just walked, following the tram rails when the street lighting failed to illuminate the pavements. Smog also blackened the city's many fine buildings and impaired its citizens' health.

On wide stretches of road trams could, with a following wind, attain speeds up to 55mph. Unfortunately they didn't have speedometers and drivers would end up in trouble with the Glasgow police.

Glasgow was not slow to use special trams to advertise various coming events or campaigns. Usually a tram displaying posters would be illuminated to catch the eye at night. The major mass x-ray of citizens in 1957 for TB screening was one of the campaigns for which the trams were used, as was the Scottish Industry Exhibition of 1959 in the Kelvin Hall. Passengers were not carried on these tramcars.

In very frosty conditions, a tram might jump the points and the driver had to reverse and try again. A metal cleek (the point shifter) was an essential part of the driver's equipment. It was used to shift the points where necessary. All tramcars carried sand which could be dropped on the rails, as damp weather as well as frost could make the wheels spin or skid when braking. Funnily enough, heavy rain was safer as it would wash oil or grease from the rails, whereas light rain made the rails slippier. Very occasionally, in high winds, a tramcar would even be blown over.

With the limited mobility of tramcars, a key job was that of the tram depot gateman who had to ensure that vehicles were assigned the correct 'lye' (parking space) overnight, ready for duty in accordance with the following day's timetable.

Trams did not turn round when they reached the terminus. At their destination the conductress/conductor had the job of flipping over the back rests ready for the return journey. The conductress/conductor also had to reverse the bow collector which provided the power from the overhead electrical cables. The bow current collector flipped on the tram's roof, pressing against the overhead wires. This was carried out via the drop-down window above the destination screen, where a rope could be manipulated to reverse the bow collector. Sometimes the overhead lines would break and the Transport Department's 'Tower Wagon' would be required to go out and fix the cables.

Glasgow's Argyle Street was seen as the 'tram street'. Not until the '60s were buses allowed to use

this thoroughfare; the street at times a long line of
tramcars in their fine green, cream and orange livery.

In the 1950s Glasgow's trams entered their twilight
years. They were by then considered out-dated and
inflexible, with a large proportion of the trams, tracks
and ancillary equipment nearing the end of their useful
life. The capital cost of replacing and updating the
worn-out infrastructure was seen as prohibitive.
Shortages of steel and electrical equipment were also
cited as reasons for not investing in the maintenance
required. Apart from Blackpool, Glasgow was the last
city or town in the UK to run trams until the
Manchester Metrolink opened in 1992.

The tram was a microcosm of Glasgow. All social
groups used the caurs: the elderly; young people; parents
with children; shoppers laden with purchases; shipyard
workers in bunnets; city gents in bowler hats (they would
usually travel on the lower deck saloon, not wishing
to mix with the hoi polloi upstairs). For Glaswegians,
travelling on rails provided a friendly intimacy and
sense of security as passengers sat chatting or reading
their newspapers.

Many men had come back from both World Wars
having taken up smoking. American movies had also
encouraged people to adopt the habit as it was at that
time seen as sophisticated. Smoking on the trams was
restricted to the upper deck. Any non-smokers who, in

order to get a seat, were forced to sit upstairs could find themselves lost in a thick fug of blue smoke.

Apart from the smell of tobacco, chips and beer, the trams did have a homely, unique aroma, which many Glaswegians still fondly remember to this day.

In the 1960s rapid change was made in the way of life within Glasgow, not always for the better. Motorways were built, tenement life in many areas ended, buses ruled the road, and the beloved trams were gone.

The Passing o' the Midnight Tram

There were tipsy pals sae happy,
Bawlin' oot 'Auld Glesca toon',
There were lovers in the corner,
Feelin' everythin' wis fine.
An' folks tae see aff a sodger,
Singing 'For Auld Lang Syne',
On the dear auld midnight caur.

It usually was crooded oot,
Wi' mony drunks a' roarin'.
An' mony saw it flying past,
When rain wis steady pourin'.
Still mony mair'll always mourn,
An' remember wi' nostalgia,
The dear auld midnight caur.

ANON

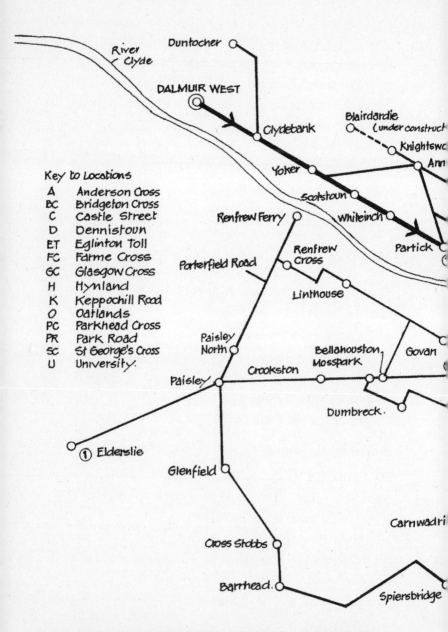

Milngav

River Clyde

Duntocher

DALMUIR WEST

Clydebank

Blairdardie
(under construct

Knightswo

Yoker

Ann

Scotstoun

Whiteinch

Renfrew Ferry

Partick

Key to Locations

A   Anderson Cross
BC   Bridgeton Cross
C   Castle Street
D   Dennistoun
ET   Eglinton Toll
FC   Farme Cross
GC   Glasgow Cross
H   Hynland
K   Keppochill Road
O   Oatlands
PC   Parkhead Cross
PR   Park Road
SC   St George's Cross
U   University

Renfrew Cross

Porterfield Road

Linthouse

Paisley North

Bellahouston Mosspark

Govan

Crookston

Paisley

Dumbreck

① Elderslie

Glenfield

Carnwadri

Cross Stobbs

Barrhead

Spiersbridge

GLASGOW CORPORATION TRAMWAY SYSTEM
SCHEMATIC DIAGRAM · NOT TO SCALE

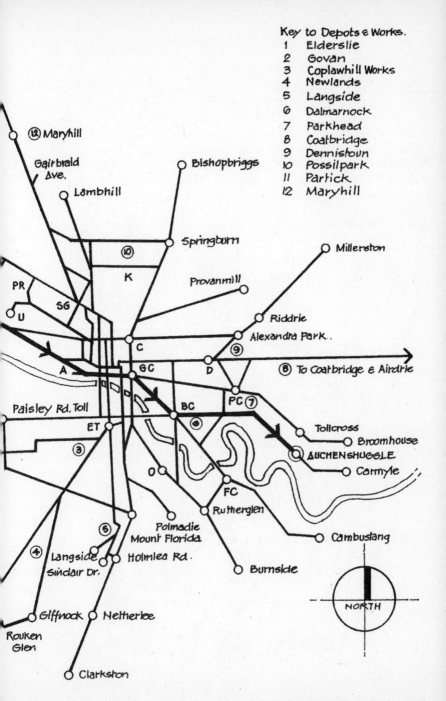

Key to Depots & Works.
1 Elderslie
2 Govan
3 Coplawhill Works
4 Newlands
5 Langside
6 Dalmarnock
7 Parkhead
8 Coatbridge
9 Dennistoun
10 Possilpark
11 Partick
12 Maryhill

⑫ Maryhill
Gairbraid Ave.
Lambhill
Bishopbriggs
Springburn
⑩
K
Millerston
Provanmill
PR
SG
U
Riddrie
Alexandra Park
C
⑨
A
GC
D
⑧ To Coatbridge & Airdrie
Paisley Rd. Toll
BC
PC ⑦
ET
Tollcross
③
Broomhouse
⑥
AUCHENSHUGGLE
O
Carmyle
FC
Rutherglen
Polmadie
Mount Florida
Cambuslang
⑤
④ Langside
Holmlea Rd.
Sinclair Dr.
Burnside
NORTH
Giffnock
Netherlee
Rouken Glen
Clarkston

RONALD SHERIDAN · RIBA · RIAS · ARB

Big Aggie's Tramlines

The lady, a regular passenger from Bearsden, had a 'cut-glass' voice. She was always full of airs and graces. The woman explained to Big Aggie that her husband was an expert on wine.

'In fact,' she commented, 'he is a founder member of the local wine club.'

'Is that the wan that meets in the park every mornin' aboot nine o'clock?' observed Aggie.

❖ ❖

'See when the trams finish in September, Aggie,' ventured a regular passenger on the number 9. 'Ur youse gonny get a job on they wans in Blackpool?'

'Me? Naw.' replied Aggie. 'Ah wid never go south o' the mince an' totty line.'

❖ ❖

'Dae ye want tae hear another o' ma wee jokes, Aggie,' asked the minister, a regular traveller to Argyle Street.

'Well, meenister, if it's anything like the last wan then ye must have goat it aff the Dead Sea Scrolls!'

❖ ❖

'Listen, you,' remonstrated the angry young man. 'Ye've gied me the wrang ticket. Ah asked fur wan tae Partick.'

'Naw! It's right,' replied Aggie. 'An' furthermore, son. Don't be smart. Jist be yersell.'

❖ ❖

'Whit dae ye dae when a passenger gets obstreperous, Aggie?' asked the small woman passenger.

'Jings, that's a big word fur a wee wummin,' replied Aggie. 'Anyway, tae answer yer question, ah boot their erses an' pit them aff at the next stoap.'

'An' whit dae ye dae if ye cannae get the fare?'

'Och, ah jist take the first two weeks in August.'

❖ ❖

'See when ye hear the bells at Hogmanay, Aggie. Does it no' bring a lump tae yer throat?'

'The only thing that brings a lump tae ma throat are the bones oot the fish suppers fae that chippie in Stockwell Street.'

❖ ❖

'Listen, Aggie. Wid it no' be nice if you could provide some sort of refreshments on the caurs?'

'Whit dae ye think this is? Meals oan Wheels!'

❖ ❖

'Listen, Aggie,' observed the passenger. 'Ah know times are hard, but ma auntie in Springburn brought up a family of 12 wi' one hand.'

'That's nothing,' replied Aggie. 'Ma feyther had 15 children an' ma mither said he wis haunless!'

❖ ❖

'Aggie, sure a lot o' auld folks aye travel oan the Glesca trams.'

'Sure. Well, it's nice and warm an' safe oan a tram.'

'Aggie, see if somebuddy beside me dies oan a tram, whit wid ah dae?'

'Easy! Move tae anither seat.'

❖ ❖

The tram stopped at the caur stop. Two drunks peered in and spied Aggie.

One of them asked, 'Hey missus, wull this tram take me tae Paisley Road?'

'Naw, it wulnae,' replied Aggie.

After a few seconds the other drunk asked, 'Whit aboot me?'

Big Aggie turned to passengers sitting near the platform and observed. 'Sure ye couldnae make it up.'

❖ ❖

The young lady was telling Aggie about her latest beau. 'He lives in Bearsden. He has a great job and drives a sports car. It's his birthday next week, Aggie. Whit would you give a man who has everything?'

'Encouragement, hen. Encouragement!'

❖ ❖

'Nice wee wean you've goat there,' remarked Aggie to the young girl holding the baby wrapped in a shawl around her shoulder.

'Aye, she's a lovely wee thing. But ah've telt ma man, nae mair. Ah wis 18 hours in labour. Murder it wis.'

'Tell me aboot it, hen! When ah had ma first ah ended up wi' over 20 stitches. Ah could've walked doon baith sides o' Sauchiehall Street at the same time.'

❖ ❖

'Aggie, you know aw the tram ticket prices, sure ye do. Whit's the best way tae get a right guid run fur yer money?'

'Go tae that new Indian restaurant oan the High Street.'

❖ ❖

Aggie had a persistent admirer, an older man who always waited until her number 9 caur came along. This time he was pushing his luck. 'Ah love big, vibrant wummen, Aggie. You know ah've always fancied you. Whit aboot it? Tonight, your place or mine?'

'Both! You go tae yours and ah'll go tae mine.'

As Aggie turned and swayed down the aisle, a passenger who had overheard the encounter asked, 'Dae ye no' fancy him, then, Aggie?'

'Let me tell you, ah'd rather be tied tae a coo's tail an' skittered tae death. Anywize, he's that auld he probably couldnae even raise a smile!'

❖ ❖

Mrs Brown was visiting her neighbour Mrs Bell.

'Is that a parrot you have there, Mrs Bell?'

'Aye, ah bought him yesterday. He's a rare talker. Just listen.'

At that the parrot began to talk, and true enough he was an extremely clear speaker.

'Can ah ask ye, Mrs Bell, did ye bring yer parrot hame fae the pet shop on a number 9 Auchenshuggle tram by any chance?'

'Aye, ah did. How dae ye know?'

'Well, it's the first time ah've heard a parrot say, 'Ferrs, pal-eeze. Ferrs-pal-eeze. Ur ye getting' a hook an' a widden leg next, missus?'

The lady who had boarded the tram at Scotstoun displayed a superior air. She told Aggie all about her family's achievements. Then added, 'I have got to tell you, conductress, that my husband and I actually met in a private establishment.'

'Wis it recommended by a judge?'

❖ ❖

'Aggie, ur ye no' pleased that the trams are stopping soon? Dae ye no feel age creepin' up on ye?'

'Listen. The only thing that creeps up oan me is ma knickers.'

❖ ❖

'Sit doon an' behave yersell. Yer drunk, ya silly auld fool. You'll fall aff the caur,' shouted Aggie at the passenger, clearly the worse of drink.

'Hey, you. No woman ever made a fool o' me.'

'Did ye dae it aw yersell, then?'

❖ ❖

The somewhat sour faced man held out his money and grunted, 'Yoker.'

Aggie gave him his ticket and change. The man lingered long over checking the money.

'Is yer change no' right,' demanded Aggie.

'Aye,' he replied. 'Just.'

Aggie's hackles went up and she retorted. 'An' that's as good as it's goin' tae get, sunshine!'

'Aggie, some o' the trams are in a bit o' a state. Ah wis oan an auld Standard caur yesterday and it wis over 50 years old. In fact sumbuddy had written oan the dirt on the side, 'Rust in Peace'. Ah mean, ur they still safe tae go oan?'

'Aye, they're perfectly safe,' replied Aggie. 'Anyway, they're insured by Glesca Corporation against fire and Viking raids.'

❖ ❖

The young woman was skinny, very skinny. Like so many others she poured out her troubles to Aggie.

'The problem is ah'm like a tramcar, Aggie. Ah look the same fae the back and the front. Ye see, ah've nae front tae speak of, an' ma shoulder blades stick oot the back. Whit ah'm ah gonny dae tae get a man?'

'Easy,' smiled Aggie. 'Get yersell a pair o' glasses, then the lads will know which way yer facin'.'

Big Aggie and Strong Drink

It suddenly swung into view in the distance. It came on steadily without any slackening of pace, the shimmering light of the hot July afternoon gleaming from its dignified body. She became aware of the noise; a steady hum rising in volume. As it came near she recognised that all trace of newness had long since gone. The grime of years was beaten into the metal. It was worn, stained and patched, yet a kind of enduring magnificence remained.

Her hypnotic fascination was broken as it screeched to a halt. A face appeared. The impact was immediate. 'Get yer weary erse oan quick, Maisie. We're runnin' late!'

'Oh, it's yersell, Aggie,' said the waiting passenger as she climbed quickly onto the tram platform.

'Aye, it's me, Maisie. We were held up fur ages at Kelvingrove Art Gallery. A big tar boiler had burst on the road, and we jist goat past before it started tae solidify. See they tarmacadam boilers wi' their big lang chimneys, they're dangerous things. But ah huv tae say ah like the smell o' boiled tar. Ma sister's whoopin' cough was helped by the smell o' the stuff, ye know. Mind you, ah don't know what will happen tae the caurs behind us. They'll no' be able to run.'

'That explains it,' said Maisie. 'Your tram wis the only wan comin' alang. Ah though it wis odd.'

'Then,' continued Aggie, somewhat annoyed that Maisie had interrupted her flow of talk, 'a bunch o' tourists fae London were dithering whether or no' tae come on. It took furever fur them tae make up their minds. Noo they're takin' up half ma tram. An' ye widnae believe it, they cannae understaun' whit ah'm saying. Ah mean, whit kind o' education dae they gie them in London? Thank goodness oor schools learn us proper up here.'

'Yer right, Aggie,' agreed Maisie. 'Dae ye know ah wis wance in London masell an' ah couldnae understaun whit *they* were saying.'

Maisie looked around. 'Aggie, ah'll need tae go upstairs. Aw the seats are taken on yer lower deck an' ah'm no' fit enough tae staun.'

'Aye, right enough, Maisie, yer lookin' a wee bit peely-wally. But don't worry, Maisie, haud on an' ah'll get ye a seat.'

Aggie searched the lower deck and identified a young man sitting near the door. 'Right, you. Up sunshine! Gie this nice auld woman yer seat.' The young fellow looked up, was about to question the request, but the glint in Aggie's eyes clearly conveyed the message. He stood.

'Sit doon, Maisie. Ah wid chat tae ye but ah've goat

a few mair ferrs to collect an' ah heard that wee toerag, Inspector Campbell, is on the prowl the day. Ye wid think he wouldnae be caring wi' the trams finishing soon. But no, his majesty loves the power. As far as ah'm concerned he's jist a pimple on a camel's what-not. Anyway, efter September he'll be as important as the rest o' us.'

'Ferrs, pal-eeze. Ferrs, pal-eeze,' shouted Aggie, a handful of pennies jingling in her hand while she forged her way up the aisle of the lower deck of the shoogling caur, standing passengers parting like waves before her relentless progress.

Further up the tram a well-dressed lady and her son were seated. 'One and a half, conductress.' came a commanding voice.

'Missus,' replied Aggie, looking intently at them both. 'that boy o' yours is 16 if he's a day.'

'I'll have you know, conductress, I've only been married 12 years.'

'Listen, hen,' replied the redoubtable Aggie. 'Ah'm only takin' ferrs. No' confessions.'

'How dare you, conductress, imply that I have been anything less than honourable in the past!'

'Implying nothing! It's as clear as the nose oan ma face. Anyway, yer boy is wearin' lang trousers. He would need tae be wearing short troosers.'

'In that case, conductress,' said the woman, with a sly smile. 'I'll have the half fare.'

At that a young lady across the aisle piped up. 'If that's the way it is then ah want ma money back!'

Aggie growled, 'Listen you lot. Behave yerselves! It doesnae matter whither ye're wearin' lang pants, short pants or nae pants, ye'll aw pay the right fare!'

With a 'tut' and a dirty look, the woman handed over the correct cash for her son and herself. When Aggie came back down the aisle she observed to Maisie, 'Ye cannae be up tae them ye know. Up to every trick in the book so they are. But they'll no' beat me.'

'Ye didnae take ma fare, Aggie.'

'Aye, ah did,' responded Aggie with a wink. 'An' if the inspector comes on ah'll even gie ye a ticket.'

'Thanks, Aggie.'

'Well, ah've got tae look efter ma auld school pals, sure ah have?'

'The old school tie, Aggie, eh?'

'No' wi' the school we were in! Naebuddy could afford a tie.'

'Och it wis a great school, Aggie. Sure the classes were that big by the time they had finished callin' the register it wis aboot time tae gae hame.'

The number 9 continued on its journey along Argyle Street before coming to an erratic, sudden stop under the 'Hielanman's Umbrella', the bridge leading into the Central Station. Aggie barged up front to remonstrate with Jimmy Tamson, the driver. 'Hey, whit's the game, Jimmy. Ye nearly sent me an' the hale lot o' the passengers flying. Wur ye testin' yer brakes or something?'

'Naw, naw, Aggie. Somethin' is wrong. Ma wheels must have jammed.'

'Well, ye were goin' at a fair old lick afore we stopped. Must have been doing 25 miles an hour at least.'

'Aggie! Ah wis hardly moving. Honest. Maybe doing ten or even five miles per hour.'

'Listen, Jimmy, in a minute ye'll be telling me the caur wis reversing!'

'It's that tar we went over back on Dumbarton Road. Ah bet you that's the cause.'

'Well, whether it is or no', look who's jist jumped oan. Herr Muller of the Gestapo himsell tae gie us hassle, nae doubt.

All five feet nuthin' o' him, an' it looks as though sumbuddy has stolen his scone. Oh, haud oan! Ah've jist remembered, ah need tae gie a certain passenger a ticket.'

Aggie scrambled back down the tram only to find that the Inspector had already started to check the passengers' tickets, and her friend Maisie was sitting with her mouth wide open clearly trying to think of something to say.

'Hullo, Inspector. Awfa nice tae see yer cheery wee dial.'

'Mrs MacDonald,' droned Inspector Campbell. 'This passenger does not have a ticket, and she tells me she had been on your vehicle for at least ten minutes. Your tram seems in disarray.'

'Naw, Argyle Street, Inspector.'

'Sorry, Aggie,' interrupted Maisie. 'Ah've let you down.'

Addressing Maisie, Campbell enquired, 'Are you a friend of the conductress, madam.'

'Uh-huh,' replied Maisie sheepishly.

'This is extremely serious, Mrs MacDonald. I will have to report you to your depot manager. You will probably be on a 'ten o'clock line' to appear in front of the Senior Inspector. I am sure the consequences will be unfortunate to say the least. I would guess a dismissal. And,' he continued in his didactic tone, 'your vehicle has been stationary for sometime, Mrs MacDonald. It is our public duty to convey the public to their correct destination in an appropriate manner, and in keeping with our timetable.'

'Sounds as if that's right oot the rule book, Inspector. Ye must hae a great memory.'

'Oh, I do, Mrs MacDonald. I remember each of the many occasions that we have conversed.'

'Aye, sure it's great tae have nice memories, Inspector.'

'Mrs MacDonald, as a servant of the great Glasgow Corporation it is my fervent duty to ensure that all trams run properly and all passengers pay the appropriate fares.'

'An' yer daein' a grand job, Inspector.'

'My superiors think so, Mrs MacDonald.'

'Ah'm glad sumbuddy thinks... eh, ah mean ah'm glad sombuddy up there does. If yer here tae help, Inspector, ye better see ma driver. The bleedin' tram's stuck.'

'Stuck?'

'Aye, wi' tar pit doon by your great Glasgow Corporation on the roads. No doubt in preparation fur aw they buses they will be operating.'

'Leave this to me, Mrs MacDonald. I'll sort this out.' And Inspector Campbell disappeared outside the tram.

Immediately Aggie heard a clatter and a scream. All the London tourists stared out astonished to see the figure of the Inspector lying on the road, a cyclist and bike on top of him. Aggie was first off. She helped the cyclist to his feet then knelt down beside the stricken inspector who was lying prone on the cobbles.

'It wisnae ma fault,' protested the cyclist. 'He just

ran oot fae yer tram an' ah couldnae help hitting him. Ah hope ah huvnae killed him.'

'That's no' whit ah'm hopin', son,' murmured Aggie.

Jimmy appeared on the scene. 'Jings, Campbell disnae look o'er good. We had better get him intae a shop an' maybe phone an ambulance. Better still, there's a pub right here. Mind you we'll need tae be awfa careful as we're no' really supposed to go intae pubs wi' oor uniform on. But, this is an emergency.'

With Aggie, Jimmy and the cyclist all helping, Inspector Campbell was lifted through swing doors

into the Hielanman's Vaults. The pungent smell of stale
beer, tobacco and sawdust immediately hit them.
The place was full of men, conversation at a high pitch.
Two barmen in long white coats looked up from where
they stood behind the bar. Then the hubbub slowly
died as the cloth-capped drinkers turned and looked
at this intrusion, as Inspector Campbell was laid out
on a bench seat against a wall.

One of the barmen, a tall, handsome fellow with dark
wavy hair and a moustache came over. He addressed
Aggie, whose eyes flickered as she took in his looks.
'Listen, conductress, women usually drink next door
in the snug, you know.'

'It's an emergency,' Aggie explained. 'This tram
Inspector has been run o'er by a bike, ye see.'

'It wisnae ma fault,' interrupted the distraught cyclist.
'He jist appeared aff a caur. Didnae even look where he
wis going.'

'Well, he doesnae look so hot,' agreed the barman.

'Maybe a wee refreshment would help him,'
suggested Jimmy.

'Ah'll soon get a wee dram fur him if ye like,' said
the barman. 'But who's gonnae pay fur it? Oor gaffer is
a right stickler fur charging every drap.'

'Tell ye whit,' said Aggie, lookin' directly at Jimmy
with a conspiratorial glance. 'Mak it a double, an' ah'll
pay fur it.'

A large whisky was duly brought, by which time the inspector was starting to come round. He protested he couldn't possibly take strong drink as he was teetotal.

'Pit it in a pint glass an' fill it up wi' American Cream Soda or any other ginger,' Aggie whispered to the barman. 'Then he'll no' know whit's in it.'

The pint glass, full to the brim, was duly delivered. When held to his lips the contents were thirstily consumed by Inspector Campbell.

'Ah still think we need tae call a doctor,' said Jimmy.

'Naw, naw,' said Aggie with a wink. 'It is oor duty tae report this. Tell them it's awfa serious, both wi' Inspector Campbell's wee accident and the caur being stuck. If ye ask me this whole situation needs attention fae the high heid yins.'

'Yer right,' replied a grinning Jimmy.

Inspector Campbell lay back, eyes closed, on the bench cushions, recovering from his trauma while Jimmy used the pub's phone to call Head Office.

While they were waiting Aggie went outside to the tram. She lit a cigarette and took a drag, then hissed the smoke out through determined lips. All of the passengers had got off, sensing it would be a while before this particular number 9 moved again. Then she became aware that Maisie was still on board, sitting with a sad, mournful face.

'Ah'm awfa sorry, Aggie, ah didnae mean tae get ye

intae trouble. Ah'm black affronted. Ah wis taken aback, ye see. He's such an officious wee man that Inspector fella.'

'Don't you worry, Maisie. Nae bother. But ah want ye aff this caur right noo. We might have some o' the Corporation officials cummin' tae inspect it, and it would be better if you skedaddled, heap pronto. In fact here comes the polis, too.'

'Okay, ah'll away. See you later, Aggie.' And Maisie disappeared into a pavement thronged with folk.

'Is there a problem with this tramcar, conductress?' asked the beat policeman. 'It seems it hasn't moved for quite a while.'

Aggie quickly explained the situation and the constable then disappeared into the pub to investigate further, followed by Big Aggie.

Hardly had she re-entered the pub when a couple of tram officials appeared from their patrol van, their uniforms immaculately pressed and buttons gleaming. She recognised them as 'Frog Face' Ferguson and his cohort 'Toady' Thomson, the fearsome 'Gestapo'. 'A right pair if ever there was. Couldna run a menodge,' murmured Aggie.

Together with the policeman they gathered round Inspector Campbell who, somewhat incoherently, gave them his version of events. Next the cyclist was questioned and finally Jimmy and Aggie. At this point

the Corporation officials left to inspect the tram. The barman nodded to the policeman, and in no time the law was standing at the bar having a wee refreshment, on the house. The rest of the drinkers gave him a wide berth.

Five minutes later the 'Gestapo' returned. 'Frog Face' spoke to Aggie and Jimmy in a somewhat Kelvinside accent. 'Inspector Campbell has given us a story of a passenger without a ticket and the wheels of the tramcar being stuck. However, in view of the confusing

circumstances, and even although you are in unform in a public place, and as the Inspector in such an, em, well, unfortunate state, it is best we overlook this event. You two get along back to the depot, and you can cash up, conductress. We will radio for the breakdown wagon as we must clear the line outside as soon as possible.'

When the duo got back to the depot they were given bad news. Apparently Inspector Campbell had recovered and would be back on duty the following day.

As Aggie and Jimmy now had some free time, and as it was still warm, they decided to meet at the Heilanman's Vault snug for a small refreshment. Two hours later, and now dressed in their 'civvies', they met up at the pub. The stuck tram had long since been removed and Argyle Street's caurs were running normally once more.

The following morning, at the start of the day's shift, they both reported to the depot looking some-what bleary-eyed.

'See last night, Aggie,' mumbled Jimmy, 'ah think ah overdid it a wee bit. Wan mair pale ale and ah would've been under a table.'

'Listen, Jimmy. Wan mair dram an' ah would've been under that good lookin' barman!'

Big Aggie's Tramlines

It was Aggie's last shift on a Friday night. 'Hey conductress,' asked the pompous drunk. 'Wi' that heavy uniform huv ye ever been mistaken fur a man?'

'Naw. Have you?'

❖ ❖

The man was giving Aggie his worries. 'Ye see, ma heid's fair burstin'. Ah'm that up tight. If ah had a gun ah wid shoot ma brains oot.'

'Ye'll need tae be an awfa good shot, mister.'

❖ ❖

Being Glasgow, passengers were inclined to chat. A regular was telling Aggie that she had 'lost' her man a couple of years ago. 'Dae ye ever think o' the hereafter, an' dyin', an' things, Aggie?'

'Naw, dying disnae worry me. Mind ye the next day ah'll probably be a wee bit stiff.'

❖ ❖

The well-dressed, middle aged lady waltzed onto the tram, obviously in high spirits. Aggie could not help herself. She commented, 'Ye seem tae be oan tap o' the world the day, missus.'

'Aye, ye see… I'm having an affair,' she confided in a whisper.

'Lucky you. Is the Co-operative daein' the caterin'?'

❖ ❖

'It's terrible the sacrifices some folks have had to make fur their country,' observed a talkative passenger. 'Ma grandfather was injured in the Great War, and do you know he ended up wi' a wooden leg.'

'Och, that's nothin',' replied Aggie. 'Ma grandfeyther had an oak chest.'

❖ ❖

'Excuse me, conductress,' asked the disembarking passenger. 'Where wull ah find the Barras?'

'Probably where ye left them!'

❖ ❖

'Hey, Aggie, you an' that driver o' yours have been thegither quite a while on a number of routes. You seem tae hae a sweet an' simple relationship.'

'Aye, he's simple an' ah'm sweet!'

❖ ❖

The caur was full and Aggie rang the bell for it to move off from the stop. A young man who had given Aggie hassle in the past came running up behind, 'Hey,' he shouted. 'Wait, wait!'

As the tram picked up speed Aggie shouted, 'Fifteen stones but ah'm tryin' tae lose a few pounds!'

❖ ❖

'Oh, yes, conductress,' said the swanky lady in the fur coat. 'I was brought up in a house which had stained glass windows.'

'Me tae, hen,' replied Aggie. 'It wis they bleedin' pigeons oot ma feyther's doo hut that kept shittin' oan them.'

❖ ❖

'See her, Aggie. You know, the wan at the front o' the tram wi' teeth stickin' oot her mooth like shovels ootside an ironmonger's door. Well, she's always at the doctor, so she is. Always got something wrang wi' her. She told me the doctor now says she has a flower allergy.'

'Obviously a bloomin' idiot,' agreed Aggie.

❖ ❖

'Ferrs, pal-eeze. Ferrs, pal-eeze. Right missus where are ye going?'

'A'm no' sure.'

'Yer no' sure? Well, is it Argyle Street, Dumbarton Road, Yoker, Clydebank or whit?'

'A'm still no' sure.'

'Listen, missus. If ye don't know where yer going how will ye know when ye get there?'

❖ ❖

Aggie was up in front of the Chief Inspector. A passenger had reported her for throwing him off her tram.

'Did you or did you not, Mrs MacDonald,' asked the Chief Inspector, 'throw this man off your number 9 to Auchenshuggle?'

'Aye, ah did. He wis being abusive.'

'But Mrs MacDonald,' replied the Chief Inspector, 'I have personally talked to this passenger and have got to say that he is a man of few words.'

'Aye, well he gave me the benefit o' two o' them!'

❖ ❖

The two older ladies got onto the tram at Yoker. One of the women had a bandage round her jaw. 'Ye see, Aggie,' she explained. 'Wilma here tripped the other day and fractured her jaw.'

'Sorry, to hear that,' replied Aggie.

'Aye' continued the woman, 'and noo she cannae bite oan her bottom wi' her upper teeth.'

'Och,' said Aggie, 'jist tell her tae gie it a wee scratch noo an' again.'

❖ ❖

It was Friday night and Aggie was getting hassle from an 'over refreshed' gentleman.

'See you, conductress, ye'r beyond a joke.'

'Aye, an' you're beyond yer stoap, sunshine. Aff! O-F-F, aff!'

❖ ❖

It was late Friday night and the tram had squealed to a stop. Aggie came downstairs to find a drunk urinating off the platform.

'Hey, ye cannae dae that!' shouted Aggie.

'Ah'm only pishin' oan the street, missus.'

Aggie's boot swung and landed on the drunk's backside. He immediately fell off.

The drunk gathered himself together an' shouted, 'Hey, whit did ye dae that fur?'

'Ye wanted tae pish oan the street. On ye go, ya eejit. But ye'll no' get oan ma tram the next time *you're* pissed!'

❖ ❖

The regular traveller got onto the tram at Partick. She had great difficulty as her arm was in plaster. Aggie got down and helped her on.

'Thanks, Aggie. It's been difficult wi' this stookie. Ye see ah broke ma arm in two places.'

'Well, ah widnae go tae those two places again,' replied Aggie.

'Your weather's terrible here in Glasgow,' observed the English visitor, glancing out of the tram window at the pouring rain. 'And it's also very wet and steamy in this tramcar.'

'Uch, oor weather has great advantages,' said Aggie defensively.

'What advantages?'

'Well, it maks it easy fur Glesca folks tae start up conversations.'

❖ ❖

'Ma wee boy wants tae be a tram driver when he grows up, Aggie.'

'Well, ah'm awfa sorry tae say that in a couple o' months the trams will be finished.'

'Oh, ah forgot. Maybe he'll want tae be a bus driver.'

'Aye, well you shouldnae stand in his way.'

❖ ❖

'Hey, conductress. Ah nearly fell gettin' oan this tram at Bridgeton Cross. Ah could have broken ma leg. There's a big hole in the street.'

'Don't you worry, dearie. Ah'll get the Corporation tae look intae it.'

❖ ❖

'Wis that wee Inspector Campell oan yer tram there?
Ah think ah saw him gettin' aff when ah wis gettin' oan.'

'Aye, it wis the wee man himself, aw right. Full of
complaints and ideas how ah can improve ma duties.'

'So whit ur ye gonnae dae, Aggie?'

'Nuffin'! Ah jist turn a blind ear tae that wan.'

❖ ❖

The woman at the head of the queue shouted to Aggie,
who was standing on the platform enjoying a quick fag,
'Does this tram go to the concert in St Andrew's Halls?'

'Naw. It cannae sing!'

❖ ❖

The extremely well-dressed, somewhat overbearing
man sat on the upper saloon deck. Aggie didn't like
the look of him. His eyes were a bit too close together.
'Excuse me, darling,' he said to Aggie. 'But I seem to
have come out without my lighter. I wonder if you
would oblige with a match?'

Aggie duly opened her Bluebell box of matches and
handed him one.

She had hardly turned away when she heard the voice,
'Isn't it ever so annoying. I seem to have left my
cigarettes at home. I wonder, darling… ?'

'Aye,' replied Aggie. 'Right enough. Ye had better gie
me ma match back. It's nae good tae you.' And she put
it back in the box.

As a regular woman passenger got off the tram, another lady observed to Aggie. 'Chatter, chatter, chatter, that Euphemia Smith. Wid ye no' agree, Aggie, she never shuts up?'

'Yer right. Her tongue is so lang she could seal an envelope efter she posted it in the box.'

❖ ❖

'Ah'm that sad the day, conductress. Ah'm in the doldrums.'

'Naw, yer no'. Yer oan the number 9 fae Dalmuir West.'

❖ ❖

The woman at the head of the queue shouted to Aggie. 'Is this caur goin' tae Maryhill Road?'

'Naw, Dalmuir West,' replied Aggie.

'But it doesnae say that oan the front.'

'Listen. It says Persil oan the side but wur no' takin' in washin'!'

❖ ❖

Big Aggie and The Steamie

'So whit ur ye bringin' oan the day?' Aggie asked the woman who for the last week had been transporting various items of furniture on the tram. 'It looks like a wee cabinet, this time.'

'It is, conductress. Ah'll be glad when this flittin' is o'er. The auld Standard caurs are better than they Coronations fur movin' stuff aroon. But this cabinet is awfa heavy tae get oan the caur platform. Gonnae geeza haun?'

'Nae bother. Ah jist hope it's no' gonnae be a piano tomorrow,' chuckled Aggie, getting down from the platform and helping to lift the cabinet on, then tucking it as far as it would go under the stairs. 'Anyway, can yer man no' help ye?' she wheezed.

'Naw, he's on the sick at the moment. It's his chest, ye see.'

'Well, if you keep carrying this heavy stuff around, then you'll get whit they call furniture disease. It's when yer chest ends up in yer drawers,' laughed Aggie, ringing the bell.

At the next stop a large queue was waiting to board. Aggie struggled to get everyone on board, especially with the kitchen table now on the platform. Finally she shouted, 'Right, is that everybody oan?' her hand on the bell.

'Naw. Haud oan till ah get ma claes oan,' came a shout.

'Yer claes?'

'Aye. Ma washin'.'

'Thank heavens for that,' said Aggie to a thin, weary looking woman struggling with a bundle of washing tied in a sheet. 'Fur a minute ah thought we were going tae have an interesting wee incident wi' sumbuddy in the scuddy.'

As the tram shoogled off, Aggie was kept busy collecting fares from the passengers who had just embarked. 'Ferrs-paleeze. Ferrs-paleeze. Get yer money oot ready. Wur full the day an' ah'm awfa busy.'

She had almost finished on the upper deck when Aggie came across a somewhat inebriated middle-aged man. 'Hey, conductress. Ah heard ye takin' fares. Dae ye no' think you're a bit cheeky wi' some o' the punters oan the tram? Ur yer words no' a bit cross?'

'Ah like cross words, sunshine.'

'So dae ah, but it's the crossword in the *Record* that ah like.'

'Well, if ye like words so much, here's a test fur ye. Rearrange the following words. 'Aff' an' 'bugger'!'

And so saying Aggie stomped downstairs leaving the man open mouthed.

A few stops later she saw the cabinet had disappeared. In its place was the bundle of washing.

Aggie looked around the lower deck but couldn't see the passenger who had brought on the washing. She hollered, 'Hey, whose dirty washin' is this oan the platform?' No one responded. 'Strange,' thought Aggie. 'Leaving yer washing oan a tram... ah'm no' sure whit tae dae wi' this load.'

It was only as the tram trundled along London road that Aggie's kind side kicked in, and she decided that she would do the missing woman a good turn. 'Och, she looked a puir soul,' she thought. 'Ah could hand her washin' in at the depot but it might be that her family need clean claes. There's a steamie in Helenvale Street an' wan at Bridgeton Cross but ah think there' wan near Auchenshuggle, tae. Ah'll pit it in there. If the wifie comes back ontae ma tram then ah'll tell her it's aw ready waitin' tae be washed at the steamie. In fact, ah'll see if somebuddy in the steamie could maybe wash them fur her.'

Thankfully there was eight minutes to spare at the Auchenshuggle terminus before the return journey. So once Aggie had changed the destination screen, turned the seats and pulled the bow collector over, she dashed round the corner to the steamie with the washing bundle.

At the steamie door she was hit by the smell of steam and soap. Inside was an office. A notice on the wall gave the price for a washing stall. Two shillings and sixpence.

'Are you the Jannie and is there onybuddy here who could dae this washin' fur me?' Aggie asked the man sitting in the small office reading a newspaper.

He looked up. 'Aye, ah'm the Jannie. Ma wife Rita will dae them fur ye. She's free jist noo. She works here as well, ye see. But it'll cost wan an' six.'

'Okay, that' wull be fine. So, gie's a ticket fur a stall fur yer Rita, an' here's her money, tae,' Aggie said. Then she thought, 'Jings this is unusual for me, ah'm the wan usually dishin' oot the tickets.'

'Here's yer ticket, conductress. Number 17. Jist leave yer washin' here the noo an' ah'll get oor Rita tae get it intae the stall. Ur you no' workin' the day, conductress?'

'Ah am. But sumbuddy left their dirty washing oan ma tram. Ah felt heart sorry fur the wummin. Looked awfa trachled an' downtrodden. Thought ah wid dae her a good turn. The truth is, that as ye probably know, it will no' be lang till the caurs finish fur good, an' ah think ah'm getting a bit... well... sentimental as ah've worked on them fur years, ye see. But noo ah need tae skedaddle. Oor tram is due tae leave in a minute, and ye know whit they transport Inspectors are like.'

'Look, jist give me a shillin' fur oor Rita tae dae the washin' fur ye, seeing as it's a sort o' charity case.'

'Naw, it's no' charity. She looked a proud wee

wummin. Ah jist want tae help the soul.' And Aggie dashed out the door into the fresh air. She quickly waddled over to the tram to find Jimmy anxiously looking at his pocket watch, as he nervously twirled his chain and albert.

'Sorry, Jimmy. Jist lookin' after a customer's wee problem.'

'Aggie, wan minute yer geein' the passengers grief, and the next you're aw heart. Ah think really yer jist a big safty.'

'Listen, Jimmy, get this auld tram going or ah'll gie ye a demonstration how ah deal wi' the awkward wans.'

It was relatively quiet on the return journey, Aggie scanning each caur stop they approached. Just before Bridgeton Cross Aggie saw her. Concern was written all over the woman's face.

'Ah left ma washin' oan yer tram, conductress. Ye see ah felt a wee bit sick. Ah'm expectin', it's ma seventh, so ah jist got aff the caur fur a bit o' fresh air and before ah knew it the tram wis awa. Huv ye got ma bundle?'

'Naw at the moment, hen. Ah thought ah wid dae ye a favour an' ah pit it intae the steamie near Auchenshuggle.'

'But ah wis comin' *fae* a steamie. The claes are aw washed an' dried.'

'Aw, naw! Ah didnae look. Ah shoulda known as there wis nae Fairy or ither soap wi' the bundle. Well, they're going tae be super clean noo, hen. Ye better get oan another tram going east tae Auchenshuggle an get them back.'

'Aye, an' ah'll need tae get hame soon tae make ma man's tea. Ah better jist away across the road and catch another number 9. Huv ye goat the steamie ticket?'

'Aye, here ye are. Stall 17. Sorry, missus, but ah wis jist trying tae help, ye see. At least it's paid, so that's something. Anyways, whit's yer name?'

'Maggie. But ah cannae have ye paying fur ma washin' even if it didnae need cleaned. Ah've only goat a few pennies at the moment but ah'll get the money tae ye somehow.'

'Ah don't want any money, Maggie. It wis ma mistake. Ma name's Aggie by the way. Look here's a caur comin' noo. Quick, on ye go across the road. Cheerio, ah hope ye keep well in future, Maggie.'

On the return journey from Dalmuir West to Auchenshuggle Aggie was agitated. 'Ah hope that wee wummin got hame safely. Nice wee person.' She thought. 'Ah fairly mixed that up. Me, interfering as usual!'

By the time the tram finally returned to Auchenshuggle, Aggie had got herself into a bit of a state so she decided to return to the steamie to make sure all had gone well. Inside she was surprised to find Maggie still there, talking to the janitor.

'Is everythin' no' okay?' asked Aggie anxiously.

'Naw,' replied Maggie. 'They've gied me back the wrang washin'.'

'Ah don't know how it's happened,' said the janitor. 'Ah'm fair dumfoonered. Ah gave the washin' tae oor Rita. First of all she said it wis funny cause the claes looked clean and were aw folded. But as you'd paid she washed them. Noo there seems tae be a wee mix up. Somebuddy else must have this wummin's washing and she's got theirs.' And he pointed to a bundle of washing sitting on a table nearby.

'Ur ye sure it's no' your stuff in that bundle?' asked Aggie.

'Ah jist had a quick peep inside and it's no mine. It's mainly the same kind o' claes, but newer.'

Aggie asked the janitor. 'Is it aw right if we go intae the steamie an' have a quick look roon tae see if we can spot her washing?'

'Nae bother, on ye go.'

'Don't worry, ah'll need tae be quick. The tram's waitin' fur me... as usual.'

The smell of soap mixed with sweat in the humid conditions was all pervading.

White tiles on the walls ran with moist air. Aggie and Maggie looked around the cubicles. Old prams and bogies with galvanised tin baths on top sat around. A few women were still busy in the stalls, rubber aprons and top boots protecting their everyday wear. The shrill sound of laughter rang out as they swapped the latest gossip.

Aggie and Maggie inspected the stall at number 17. Its two metal sinks were empty and clean. Only a pair of wooden tongs hung on a hook. Looking around they saw dungarees, underwear, sheets and pillowcases all hung out to dry on moveable racks. A row of large industrial spin-dryers sat against a wall. Maggie explained, 'Rita and her husband are probably the only wans allowed tae spin. Regulations, ye know.'

'Aye, tell me aboot regulations,' grunted Aggie.

'Ah cannae see mine anywhere. Sumbuddy must have taken it by mistake.' She sounded downcast.

'Well, let's go and have a wee dekko at whit is in the bundle that wis left, Maggie,' suggested Aggie.

First out was a huge pair of pink bloomers. 'Heavens,' exclaimed Aggie. "Passion killers'!' And she held them up for Maggie to see.

'Get your hands off my clothes!' came a loud voice.

Aggie and Maggie turned to see a hefty-built woman with a red face clip-clopping on high heels towards them.

'That's mine. Here's yours, I assume,' the woman said with some

disdain, throwing what turned out to be Maggie's washing towards them.

'Did you pick up this wummin's washin' by mistake?' asked Aggie. 'If you did then we need an apology. This puir soul has been distressed oot her mind because o' your mistake.'

'It was just a small error of judgement,' replied the woman. 'Anyway, I make it a point never to apologise to anybody.'

Aggie drew herself up to her full height. The chest was stuck out. The eyes burned. She moved to stand directly in front of the woman.

'Let's hear it, hen. The apology. An' a shilling fur aw the tram fares she's had tae pay.'

'Are you, erm, by any chance,' the woman asked,

suddenly anxious, 'that Big Aggie MacDonald off the trams ah hear people talkin' about?'

'That's me, hen.'

The woman's face went white. She fumbled for her purse. 'Here, take yer money. Erm, ever so sorry.'

'Aye, an' here's yer bloomers,' replied Aggie shoving them into the woman's hands.

The woman stuttered, 'Erm. Ye see ah like bloomers as they, erm, cover my nether regions.'

'Nether regions? They wid cover half o' Hampden Park.' And turning to Maisie said, 'Right, let's go, Maisie. Get oan ma tram. Ah've got masell intae enough trouble the day.'

The washing bundle shortly resumed its place on the platform of the shoogling Coronation number 9, with Maggie sitting near the door keeping an eagle eye on it.

When it came to her caur stop, Aggie helped Maggie off with her washing.

'That wis awfa good o' ye, Aggie. Thanks fur aw yer help. Ah'll just humph it hame noo, hang the claes oan the pulley, then make the tea.'

'It wis nice tae meet ye, Maggie,' said Aggie with a knowing smile. 'Cheery-bye. But let me give ye a bit o' advice. If ah wis you ah wid get a pair o' they pink bloomers. Ye know, the 'passion killers'.' And Aggie winked, then lifted her skirt to reveal an elasticated leg of pink. 'Let me tell ye, Maggie, they work!'

Big Aggie's Tramlines

'Aggie, dae you no' feel inferior when the upper crust fae the posher areas o' Glesca get oan yer caur?'

'No' me. Anyway that lot are jist a lot o' crumbs held thegither wi' dough.'

❖ ❖

'Is that a new driver ye've goat the day, Aggie?'

'Him! Useless! Haun' knitted if ye ask me. Ah mean this caur obviously runs oan rails, an' the stupid ass has goat tae stop every two minutes tae ask directions.'

❖ ❖

Aggie had to listen to the woman from Auchenshuggle moaning about her husband. 'He is so nervous, conductress. Gets up tight. It just gets on my nerves. He can't stop biting his nails. Ah don't know what to do about it.'

'Easy,' said Aggie. 'Hide his wallies.'

❖ ❖

The queue was long and the tram almost full. Aggie shouted, 'Wan inside and wan upstairs.' A woman passenger got on and entered the lower saloon deck, while a man started up the stairs lugging a heavy case. Suddenly his case burst open and the contents cascaded down. It was packets of cigarettes.

Aggie helped the passenger retrieve the cigarettes and asked, 'Wur ye goin' up tap tae smoke yersell tae death or wur ye just taking yer case tae a higher court?'

'Hey, keep quiet aboot this, conductress, if you don't mind, otherwise ah will be goin' tae a higher court,' and as he slipped Aggie a couple of packets he winked and added, 'Ah'm awa tae the Barras, ye see.'

❖ ❖

A water pipe had burst and the streets around Glasgow Cross were flooded. In his usual reckless way Jimmy the driver opted to drive right through. The result was that water splashed through the lower deck. Big Aggie was quick to react. 'Ferrs, pal-eeze! Ferrs, pal-eeze! Get yer ticket fur a sail doon the watter.'

❖ ❖

'Whit are ye daein' standing oan tap o' the seat missus? Get doon. Ye'll get hurt,' demanded Aggie.

'There's a moose runnin' aboot the flair o' this tram. Ah can hear it squeakin'.'

'Whit dae ye want me tae dae? Oil it'

❖ ❖

'Aggie, I goat a real bargain the day,' stated the lady shopper. 'I was in Arnott Simpson's and I bought a corset fur a ridiculous figure.'

'Don't tempt me, hen. Ah can think o' a number o' answers tae that wan.'

❖ ❖

The woman had brought her West Highland terrier on to the tram. It sat on the lower deck as good as gold. Then all of a sudden it began to bark. 'Excuse me conductress, but ma dug Sandy needs tae wee.'

'Well, he cannae wee on this tram,' said Aggie.

'Naw, he wilna do it oan a tram. He's a funny wee dug. He always needs a tree tae pit his leg up against.'

'Well, this is Argyle Street an' there's only wan tree oan the hale stretch, so if he can just haud oan a wee minute till we get there. It shouldna be long.'

'Only wan tree on the hale stretch o' Argyle Street?' queried the passenger. 'Ah thought there wid be plenty.'

'Naw, jist the wan. It's opposite the Park Bar. So at least yer wee Sandy will no' be barkin' up the wrang tree.'

❖ ❖

The blonde lady was busy looking into her compact mirror, applying lipstick. 'I've got to tell you, conductress, every time I pass a good lookin' fella he sighs.'

Aggie pulled a face. 'Is that wi' relief?' she asked.

The passenger was a neatly dressed, well groomed, weedy wee man. He was keen to talk and obviously a bit of a blow.

'I wouldn't tell this to everyone, conductress,' he confided, 'but for the last two years I haven't had a drink, smoked only a few cigarettes, have not gone around with women, have been going to bed early and also up again early. I worked long hours during the day with very little exercise.'

'So, when did ye get oot o' Barlinnie, then?'

❖ ❖

The candidate in the forthcoming Glasgow council elections was handing out leaflets on the tram. He said to Aggie. 'Yes, conductress, I have heard the voice of the people calling me to duty.'

'Ur ye sure it wisnae an echo?'

❖ ❖

'Aggie. See when you finish at night. Dae ye take a tram hame?'

'Naw. We're no' allowed. We have tae leave them in the depot.'

❖ ❖

A man with a dog on a lead was at the front of the queue. It jumped onto the tram platform. 'Listen Elvis, ye cannae bring yer hound dog on tae ma tram,' Aggie announced. 'Ah've already got the regulation number oan board. Wan doon the sterr an' wan up top.'

'But this isnae a dug,' protested the man. 'It's a whippit.'

'Well, ye can whippit aff this caur an' take it walkies, sunshine.'

The woman in curlers and a rain-mate was driving Aggie mad. Every two minutes she would enquire if this was her stop.

Finally the woman asked, 'How will ah know when we get to ma stop?'

'There'll be a big smile oan ma face, hen!'

'Ur ye going tae the depot boss's funeral tomorrow, Aggie?'

'Thingmyjig's funeral! Naw. Ah'm workin' that shift. Business afore pleasure is whit ah say.'

'Ah wonder whit they'll say at your funeral, Aggie?'

'Ah'll never know. Ye go a bit deef when yer deid.'

A lady got on the tram in Argyle Street. When Aggie asked for her fare she was busy putting on lipstick. 'Ye know, conductress, ah'm dreading the thought of 50.'

'Oh, whit happened then?'

❖ ❖

'Aggie. Dae ye buy yer man's claes? Ah mean, dae ye pick his suits?'

'Naw, jist his pockets.'

❖ ❖

Big Aggie Gets a Tip!

It had been an exceptionally busy day, full of awkward busybodies. Aggie was up to high doh. Now there was a bit of a kerfuffle going on. Aggie and a brazen wee woman were at it hammer and tongs.

'Let me tell you, conductress, yer face wid stop the toon clock.'

'An' yours wid mak it run.'

'Right! Ah'm thinkin' o' getting' aff your tram, ya bizzum, you. I'll maybe get anither wan.'

'Great! The next wan wull be alang in six minutes. Be under it!' And Aggie turned and went back to stand on the platform. 'Ah need a gasper,' she thought to herself. 'Ah'll jist have a wee Willie Woodbine,' and she opened a fresh packet.

As she lit up a passenger nearby turned to Aggie and said, 'Ah know that yin. She lives up oor close. A right 'Stairheid Sarah' so she is. Fights wi' everybuddy. Aye bitchin' in the kitchen', as they say.

Mind you, that's the first time ah've heard her no' gettin' the last word.'

'She might get mair than the last word next time,' growled Aggie, and she looked up the caur surprised to see that 'Stairheid Sarah' was still rooted to her seat.

The auld Standard shoogled on, clanging, swaying and shuddering as it made its way over the junction at Glasgow Cross. As the tram gave a further lurch an older man wearing a brown trilby jumped onto the platform, swung on the pole, and grabbed a strap on the lower deck of the full vehicle. Then he proceeded to move further down the aisle past the standing passengers while furtively glancing outside. When he could go no further he crouched behind a large gentleman, also being jerked back and forward by the movements of the tram.

Aggie had seen the man in the trilby jump on and singled him out immediately. In fact she knew who he was. Pushing her way up the caur she confronted him. 'It's Charlie, sure it is?'

'Aye, it's me. Oh, it's yersell, Agnes. How's it goin'?'

'No' bad. Funny tae hear ye call me by ma posh name. Ah huvnae seen ye since... well, Miss Stevenson's class at the school. 'Auld droopy-drawers' if you can remember her. Is sumbuddy chasing ye, Charlie? Have ye goat a problem fur ye seem awfa on edge?'

'Ah think the polis is efter me.'

'The polis! Heavens above.Whit have ye done in the name o' the wee man?'

'Jist taken a few bettin' lines. Got tae make a couple o' bob tae keep me going, ye ken, Agnes.'

'Ah had heard ye were a bookies runner, but ah thought betting shops were legalised last year in 1961. In fact occasionally ah put oan a wee line masel. Great fun so it is, especially when ah get a return.'

'Ye see, Agnes, ah still don't have a licence,' explained Charlie. 'So ah've got tae keep wan step ahead o' the law. Ah took in a pile the day an' a couple o' polis are efter me. Some bookie must have telt them. It isnae fair. Aw they posh folks can go tae Ascot or Ayr races but the poor wee Glesca punters cannae afford tae dae it. Ah still take lines fur ma regulars an' dae a bit o' runnin' fur folks that cannae get oot the hoose. Oh, naw! Quick! There they are in the polis motor alang side the tram. Crivens, they've seen me.'

'Can ah help ye at all, Charlie?'

'Aye. Look here's a wad o' notes. Could ye stick them at the bottom o' yer bag because as sure as God made little apples this lot will search me?'

Aggie didn't hesitate. She thrust the thick bundle deep into her cash bag beneath the pile of coins, and moved down the caur away from Charlie on to the platform.

As far as she could determine the tram was still full to capacity and when it stopped at the next caur stop only one passenger got off. There was a considerable queue waiting to get on but Aggie stood on the platform and shouted 'Wan only.'

As she did so two policemen ran up to the top of the queue.

They both stepped forward only for Aggie to shout, 'Ah said wan only. Dae ye no' understaun? Wan. O-n-e. Wan!'

'We are on duty following a suspect,' wheezed a big sergeant. 'Regardless of the capacity of this vehicle you must let us on. Otherwise you could be arrested for not co-operating with the law.'

'Aye, well, if that is the way then ah suppose ye better come oan, sergeant,' replied Aggie reluctantly.

'We will, conductress. Please do not ring for the tram to move on otherwise you may be in breach of the total number of passengers allowed on this vehicle. But we need to search for a man seen boarding this very tramcar.'

Aggie left them to it, and as the tram was stationary she decided to sit half way up the stairs, opened her poke of sweets and extracted a soor ploom.

The two policemen then looked into the lower deck, and seeing their suspect, pushed their way past the standing passengers until they came to Charlie, who was unsuccessfully trying to maintain a low profile.

'Sur, we have reason to believe you are illegally

operating a gambling business without the authority of the Gaming Board. Is this correct?'

'Naw me, officer.'

'Empty your pockets, sur,' instructed the sergeant.

Charlie duly turned out his pockets. Out came a comb, a dirty hankie, a newspaper folded over at the racing section, a packet of Capstan cigarettes, some loose matches, ticket stub for the cinema, a half-crown and a sixpence.

'So, sur, where's the money you took in today from the big race at Ayr?' demanded the now red-faced sergeant. 'Come on, hurry up, we know you've got a pile of cash. We're led to believe you're an illegal bookie.'

'Sure ah like the gee-gees, officer, but ah'm innocent, honest.'

'I saw him pass notes to the conductress on this tram jist two minutes ago, officer,' came the voice of 'Stairheid Sarah'. 'She stuck them in her money bag.'

'Naw, ah didnae,' protested Charlie. 'Yer eyes need tested.'

'Believe me, it's true. Ma eyes are fine. Ah never tell a lie!'

The big sergeant turned to his constable. 'Stay here, Brian, I'll investigate this.'

So saying the sergeant made his way back to the platform where Aggie was sitting on the stairs sucking her sweet.

'Conductress, we have a witness who says she saw you put money from our suspect into your money bag.'

'Oh, aye. That'll be that 'Stairheid Sarah'. Cannae believe a word that wummin says.'

'I require to inspect your money bag, conductress.'

'Huv ye goat a search warrant, sergeant?'

'I don't need a search warrant. The Glasgow police expect that all innocent parties will willingly co-operate with them. I am confident your superiors would agree with that.'

'Well, ah'm innocent. So ah'll expect an apology. Here's ma cash bag.' Aggie swung it off her shoulders and gave it to the policeman.

He put the heavy bag down on the tram deck, lifted the flap and looked inside. Putting his hand in, he rummaged through the coins at the bottom of the satchel.

Aggie stood glowering, then muttered. 'Well, Dixon o' Dock Green, whit did ah tell ye. Nothin' but coins fur fares. Where's ma apology?'

'There does seem tae be a misunderstanding here, conductress. Sorry to put you to this bother.'

'Always ready tae assist the polis, so ah am,' replied Aggie. 'Nae hard feelings. Here, have a soor ploom.' And she popped a sweet into his mouth.

The big sergeant made his way back up the aisle on the caur's lower deck. He addressed himself to a sweating Charlie. 'Ah don't know how ye did it, but let me tell you we wull be keeping a close eye on you in future. That is a warning.'

He then turned his attention to 'Stairheid Sarah'. 'Madam, I suspect you have deliberately misinformed the police in their line of duty. This is a serious offence so I need to take your name and address, and to inform you that your conduct will be reported to the Procurator Fiscal.'

The woman went white, but quietly gave her details, which the constable duly entered into his notebook.

Before they left the tram, the sergeant had one more word with Charlie. 'We are giving you a tip. Stay away from illegal betting in future, otherwise you'll end up with a heavy fine and even jail.'

'Well, if you two are giving me a tip,' said a relieved Charlie, 'let me return the favour. Here are two certs for tomorrow's meeting at Ayr. Back Glue Factory and Sotally Tober an' make yersel some dough.'

As the police officers left the tram Aggie stood, a sympathetic smile on her face, and with an offering of further soor plooms from her wee poke. Then she rang the bell, much to the relief of the passengers and those in the trams behind.

At the next stop the sulking figure of 'Stairheid Sarah' quietly slipped off the tram. Charlie stayed on until the terminus at Auchenshuggle.

Once all the remaining passengers had disembarked

at the terminus and Aggie had attended to her duties, an anxious Charlie approached Big Aggie, 'Where is ma wad o' notes, Agnes? Have ye still goat it?'

'Turn yer back an' ah'll get it oot fur ye.' Aggie's hand went into her ample bosom and, after rearranging the contents of her bra, returned clutching the money. 'Here ye are. Ah thought ah better dae a switch, just in case sumbuddy saw me take the dough. Trust it tae be that 'Stairheid Sarah'. Noo ye better be oan yer way, Charlie, or ah'll be visiting ye in the jile or even joinin' ye there.'

Charlie gave a quick look outside. No police cars were to be seen. 'Aggie, yer a real star, so let me gie ye a tip fur the three o'clock tomorrow at Ayr. Pit a couple o' bob on Real Star. Fur heavens sake don't back Glue Factory. She'll get stuck at the first fence. And definitely don't touch Sotally Tober. He'll be lucky to stagger in last!'

Big Aggie's Tramlines

'Aggie, did yer parents work on the trams, tae?'
'Naw. They were actually in the iron an' steel business.'
'My, that's impressive.'
'Aye, ma mither did ironing an' ma feyther wis forever stealing.'

❖ ❖

'How long have you been oan the caurs, Aggie?'
'Aboot 55 years.'
'How could ye work 55 years on the caurs when ye'r jist nearly 60 noo?'
'Overtime!'

❖ ❖

'Ferrs, pal-eeze! Ferrs, pal-eeze!' shouted Aggie, her left hand jingling a pile of pennies ready for change. She then stood looking down at a small man, waiting for him to speak.
'Ticket to the far end o' Argyle Street,' said the passenger.
'Naw, haud oan a wee minute, conductress. A ticket to Glasgow Cross. Naw, naw, haud oan, ah've changed ma mind.'
'Does the new wan work ony better than the auld wan?'

❖ ❖

The wee boy held out a penny for Aggie to take. She looked at him, 'Ur ye no' supposed tae say somethin'?' she asked.

He thought for a few seconds, then said, 'Gie's a ticket.'

'Listen, son, dae ye no' know there's a wee word ye should use at the start o' that sentence?'

The boy thought for another few seconds, then said, 'Gonnae gie's a ticket?'

'Can you no' add something else noo tae the start o' that?'

After a few more seconds he said. 'Ur ye no' gonnae gie's a ticket?'

Aggie's eyes narrowed. 'Look, son, here's yer ticket. Pal-eeze, pal-eeze, take it!'

❖ ❖

The woman was huge, really huge. There were no vacant seats on the lower deck and she stood holding onto a strap, her huge body swaying from side to side as the tram shoogled along.

'Ur there nae gentlemen here tae gie up their seats fur this wumman?' shouted Aggie.

Nobody moved.

Aggie tapped a wee man on the shoulder. 'Right you, up! At least ye could make a contribution.'

❖ ❖

The tram was almost empty as it shoogled along, but when Aggie came down the stairs she found three small boys swinging from roof strap to roof strap.

'Hey, ya wee monkeys. Get doon! If ye dae that again ah'll get the polis tae take ye tae Calderpark Zoo.'

❖ ❖

The lights on Aggie's tram suddenly went out and the caur ground to a halt.

'Whit's the problem?' demanded a male passenger.

'We've loast power,' Aggie replied. 'Probably the bow collector has come aff the wire.'

'This is too much,' exclaimed the passenger. 'Whit ah day a've had, nothin' goin' right, an' noo ah'm gonnae be late fur the fitba. It couldna get much worse.'

'Och, it could be worse,' said Aggie. 'Ye could be oan a plane!'

❖ ❖

'Whit dae ye think o' buses, Aggie. Wid ye no like to work on them once the trams are finished?'

'Naw, naw. Ah prefer something with rails. Ah've goat a wan track mind, ye see.'

❖ ❖

'Hey, Aggie. You've goat nice nails fur sumbuddy who handles tickets an' money all day long. Dae ye file yer nails?'

'Naw, ah jist throw them away.'

One day Aggie found a purse with money in it on the floor of the lower deck of the Auchenshuggle tram.

She announced loudly. 'Wull the person who has lost a purse with two pounds, ten shillings in it, please form an orderly queue at the next stoap.'

The man sat down in the lower deck. He held a board which said. 'Give Up Sin. Money Is The Root Of All Evil'.

Aggie read his sign, said nothing, but wrinkled her nose and raised her eyebrows.

The man explained to Aggie. 'You see, conductress, all money is tainted.'

'Well, ye see the money in ma cash bag, mister. Taint yours and it taint mine. It's the Corporation's!'

❖ ❖

The passenger at the caur stop in Partick put one foot onto the running board and enquired of Aggie. 'Hey, you. Dae ye stop at the Grosvenor Hotel at the tap o' Byres Road?'

'Naw, no' oan ma wages, sunshine.

❖ ❖

'You know, Aggie, sometimes oan a Saturday night ah feel that Glesca is a bit like the Wild West,' observed the passenger.

'Aye, yer right. Ye wid need the Glesca sheriff, Lobey Dosser, on the caurs. But oan this 'Deadwood Stage' ah'm 'Aggie get yer gun'!'

❖ ❖

'Aggie,' said the young woman, a daily passenger. 'Ah'm right worried. Somebody telt me that they saw ma husband wi' a blonde oan the beach at Millport yesterday.'

'Well, whit dae ye expect at his age?' replied Aggie. 'A bucket an' spade!'

❖ ❖

'Huv you goat false teeth, Aggie?'

'Naw, they're aw ma ain.'

'Well they look awfa good. How do you keep them in such good shape?'

'Ah mind ma ain business.'

'You! Aggie MacDonald! Minding yer ain business! Yer kiddin' me.'

'Ah dae. But everybuddy is still entitled tae ma opinion!'

❖ ❖

Two male passengers were eyeing Aggie as she collected fares on the upper deck. 'Let me tell you. Yon's a stoater. Never, ever argue wi' that wummin.'

'Is she cheeky?'

'Cheeky! The only way tae fight yon is wi' yer bunnet.'

'Yer bunnet?'

'Aye, grab it an' run.'

❖ ❖

'Aggie, have you ever been assaulted by onybuddy. Ye know, oan a late night tram oan a Saturday fur instance?' asked a passenger.

'Well, wance on a number 14 a big fella wis threatening tae banjo me. He said he wis gonnae gie me a Glesca Kiss.'

'So whit did ye dae?'

'Och, ah jist gied him two rapid wans wi' the heid.'

❖ ❖

Swaying back and forth, Aggie was on the upper deck as the tram shoogled along. A good-looking gentleman rose to pass her to make his way off. Aggie moved to the side to let him pass, and he moved to the same side. Aggie moved to the other side and again so did the man. A third attempt brought the same result.

Aggie observed, 'Listen, wan mair time then ah really must go.'

❖ ❖

Two of the lady passengers were discussing Big Aggie and her ability to stand no nonsense from anybody.

'Aye, see her. She's got a great memory, and a tongue hung in the middle o' it.'

❖ ❖

Two 'ladies of the night' got onto Aggie's tram in London Road. Aggie duly took their fares and observed, 'That you away tae report fur duty, girls?'

'Naw, we've already done oor bit fur tonight. It's too cauld staunin' wi' yer back tae a wa'.'

'Ah understaun, girls. In the tram game wi' some o' oor passengers ah've had ma back tae the wa' a few times, masell!'

❖ ❖

The woman was clearly not a Big Aggie fan. 'Hey, Big Yin, ah've goat tae say ye fairly slap aw that bright red lipstick roon yer mooth.'

'Aye, an' wi a dial like yours,' replied Aggie, 'you must use a paint roller.'

❖ ❖

'This tram always makes me late for school,' moaned the wee lad.

'Well, ah've the very answer for you, son,' said Aggie.

'Whit's that?'

'Get an earlier wan!'

❖ ❖

'Ah'm oan an' aff the trams aw day tae visit ma auld uncle in the hospital,' moaned the passenger. 'Two in the efternoon, an' two tae get back hame. Then two back tae the hospital at night and two hame. That's eight a day. Fifty-six a week. Ah'm exhausted.'

'Nae wonder,' replied Aggie sympathetically. 'If yer uncle had ony decency he wid drap deid.'

Big Aggie and Dancing

It was Friday night. Still light but dreich, with continual drizzle drifting down from a cold and damp slate-grey sky spreading puddles on uneven pavements. Glasgow city centre was awash with people clomping along through the rain, collars up, heads down, some huddling beneath umbrellas.

At a caur stop in Argyle Street a queue had formed, all trying to shield themselves from the wet, some also sheltering in nearby shop doorways. At the head of the queue was a drunk; blootered, plastered. Others in the line-up kept their distance and were relieved when they saw a brightly lit Coronation tram trundling towards them; a number 9 to Auchenshuggle. When it squealed to a halt no one got off, and the drunk only just managed to get himself onto the tram platform without falling over. To the amazement of those behind he immediately proceeded to take off his boots and jacket and was loosening his trousers as he started to crawl up the stairs.

'Whitthehellisgoinoanhere?' demanded Aggie. 'We cannae have goings oan like this.'

'Shush, hen,' slurred the drunk. 'Ah don't want ma wife an' weans tae wake up while ah'm goin' up the stairs.'

'Ya daft eejit, yer steamin'. Yer oan a tramcar. Yer

no' goin' up the sterrs in yer ain hoose. Get yer stuff
back oan this very minute, especially yer boots fur yer
feet ur mingin'. Yer lucky yer no' spendin' the night in
the jile, sunshine.'

By the time the drunk had made himself respectable
the tram had shoogled as far as Calton. Aggie dutifully
helped him off onto the street. 'Imagine that comin'
hame tae ye,' she thought. 'Ah wid swing fur him.'
She turned to the passengers sitting nearby. 'How wid
ye like tae be married tae the likes o' yon? Sure it's
diabolical.'

The words were hardly out of her mouth when a
much younger man, wearing a cheap suit and with his
dark hair dripping from the rain, stepped onto the tram,
tripped and fell.

'Sorry, miss,' he apologised. 'Ah've had a wee bit
too much tae drink, ye see.'

'Anither wan,' exclaimed Aggie. 'Wan aff an' wan
oan. Ah'm ah the only sober wan in the hale o' Glesca
the night fur heaven's sake?'

She had a good look at this one. He seemed young
and was quite good looking but his blue eyes were
tinged with red, betraying he was upset. Suddenly
Aggie's mood changed. She felt motherly. 'Okay, son,
let's have it. Whit's the matter, eh?'

He looked up at Aggie and muttered, 'Ah'm a wee
bit lost.'

'A bit lost? Ye mean a bit drunk, surely.'

'Ye see ah wis thrown oot o' Barrowland by wan o' the bouncers.'

'Ye were at the dancin' then the night?'

'Aye. Ah came up fae Greenock oan a special bus wi' a bunch o' lads and lassies fae ma work. We aw like the dancin', ye see. An' ah thought ah might see if ah could get masell a new girlfriend. Ma last wan found hersell a new lad, ye see.'

'So yer lookin' fur a lumber, then yer daft enough tae get yersell ejected fae Barrowland fur being drunk? Ah'm surprised. Ye wid be lucky tae get a glass o' orange in there. They don't serve booze.'

'Ah know. But ye see we went tae a pub first. Ah only had two strong lagers, honest. The truth is, miss, ah cannae haud ma drink, especially wi' nae food in me.'

'Ye can say that again, sunshine. Ah know fellows who can down 16 pints o' heavy an' ye widnae know.'

'Well, wan o' the bouncers spotted me. Chucked me oot. Noo ah've got tae wait till aw the rest come back oot so ah can get oan the hire bus hame.'

'So whit are ye oan this tram fur?'

'It's awfa wet and ah'm a wee bit lost. Ah thought a tram wid keep me warm and dry fur a while until it's time tae meet up wi' the others.'

Aggie looked at him closely. His face was yellow. He looked ill.

'Ye'r right, son. Ye cannae haud yer drink. Ah can see that. Whit ye need is a couple o' strong coffees in ye.'

'Aye, ah probably dae, miss.'

'Let me give ye some advice, son. We're jist aboot at Bridgeton Cross. Next tae the City Bakeries is Tambarini's café at the corner. They'll still be open. Get in there an' get coffee in ye, sober up, then get another number 9 caur back alang tae Barrowland.'

'Thanks, miss.'

'Whit's yer name, son?'

'Finlay.'

'Okay, Finlay, that's us here at Bridgeton Cross. Noo remember, get coffee doon ye and stay away fae drink in the future.'

Aggie watched as Finlay gingerly held onto the platform pole while lowering unsteady feet onto the cobbles. He looked around, spotted the café, and set off on shaky legs towards it.

A relieved Aggie rang the bell, and the tram shoogled forward along London Road towards Auchenshuggle.

'Silly wee laddie,' she muttered. 'But ah hope he's okay. He's some mother's son.'

Soon the terminus at Auchenshuggle loomed ahead, so Aggie got ready to see the few remaining passengers off before turning the seats and adjusting the destination screen and bow conductor. Then she heard a shout from the driver.

'Hey, Aggie. Where's ma poker?'

Aggie waddled up to the cab. 'Whit dae ye mean, Jimmy?'

'Ma poker, Aggie. Ye know, the point shifter tae change the rails at the crossover.'

'Well, ah huvnae touched it. If ah had it wid ah been tae use oan a drunk we had oan board twinty minutes ago. Wis it there when ye took over fae the last shift?'

'Tae tell ye the truth ah never looked. How am ah gonnae get the tram over tae the ither line?'

'Listen, Jimmy. We'll jist have tae wait till the caur behind comes up an' we can get a len o' theirs'

'Well, it shouldna be lang, Aggie. In fact ah see it comin' noo.'

The glowing interior lights of an approaching tram could now be seen, resembling a ship as it sailed smoothly towards them, stopping some 20 yards away.

'Oh, naw! Ah can see that wee pain o' an' Inspector oan that caur,' moaned Jimmy. 'He'll go daft if ah've loast ma point shifter. That wan wull no' gie up until the last tram finishes. A walkin' rule book so he is.'

'Listen, Jimmy. Ah'll go an' gie him a bit o' chat. Divert him, so to speak,' said Aggie. 'You nip o'er tae their driver an' get a wee len o' their point shifter. Hurry up noo.'

Aggie let herself down from the platform into the still falling rain, and wandered over to the other tram.

'Hullowrerr, Inspector Campbell. Howzit goin'?'

The Inspector's eyes narrowed with suspicion. His lips pinched tight as he breathed in and out through his large pointy nose.

'Mrs MacDonald, why is your driver not diverting his tram onto the other line?'

'He's jist aboot tae dae it, Inspector, but ah told him tae haud oan till ah had a wee word wi' ye. Ah thought ah wid ask ye if yer goin tae the big party that's planned at the depot, ye know the wan fur the trams finishing?'

'I have heard about it, Mrs MacDonald. But there is some time to go before that happens, you know.'

'Well, tae tell ye the truth, Inspector, ah thought it wid be nice if you an' me could maybe have a wee dance that night. Aw the crews wull be there and they aw know we've had a few wee, well, run-ins in the past, so to speak. So ye see it wid be nice if we could finish oan a friendly note. Whit dae ye say, Inspector?'

'Well, Mrs MacDonald, I, em, am touched by yer sentiments. But the problem is I am of a slightly different stature from you.'

'Don't you worry, Inspector. Efter a few jars nae-buddy wull notice.'

Just then Jimmy's tram lurched forward onto the crossover, and his voice was heard. 'Right, Aggie, we're aw ready tae go, noo.'

'And just what does that communication mean, Mrs MacDonald? Was there a problem with your vehicle?'

'Naw, naw. Ah telt him ah wis goin' tae ask ye fur a dance at the party.'

'Mmmm, ah see, Mrs MacDonald,' muttered Campbell suspiciously. 'You better be on your way. You're six minutes late,' he said glancing at his watch. 'Em, if I don't see you before I'll perhaps see you at this party... erm, Agnes.'

Aggie subsequently related the conversation to Jimmy. 'You take the biscuit, Aggie. But ah've always thought wee Campbell secretly fancied his chances wi' you. Ah heard he has an eye fur the lassies. No doubt fancies a wee cheeper.'

'A wee cheeper,' exclaimed Aggie. 'The only thing he can kiss is ma bahoochie!'

The next journey to Dalmuir West and back to Auchenshuggle was relatively uneventful. However on the next run through Bridgeton Cross Aggie got a surprise. There was the bold Finlay at the caur stop. But he wasn't on his own. His arm was round a young lady and they were busy smooching.

As the tram hissed to a halt Aggie hung out the door and exclaimed, 'By heavens, Finlay, you're a fast worker, son!'

'This is Isabella, conductress. Ah met her in the café you recommended. Ye see ah did have a few coffees

like ye said ah should, an' then Isabella came in wi' her wee sister. Well, wan thing led tae anither an' we got talkin'. So ah treated them baith tae cups o' hot peas an' vinegar.'

'Jings, you're wan o' the original big spenders!' smiled Aggie. 'Wan minute yer fleein' an' the next yer full o' caffeine. And noo ye'll soon be full o' wind!'

A long, lingerin' kiss followed before Finlay reluctantly boarded the tram. He stood looking through a window, blowing kisses, as the tram sped off.

'She fancies me, ye know,' he said proudly.

'Ah can see that,' observed Aggie. 'But she'll no fancy ye if yer aye drunk.'

'Naw, that's me finished wi' the drink noo ah'm in love. Nae need fur ony mair Dutch courage!'

'Heavens above. In love. Already! In aboot two an' a half hours. That wis quick.'

'Aye. She's gonny go tae Barrowland next Saturday an' has promised tae dance aw night wi' me.'

'Good fur you, son. Funnily enough ah've promised a dance tae sumbuddy masel the night, an' ah cannae wait!'

And Aggie pulled a face.

Big Aggie's Tramlines

The Glasgow councillor got on the tram at Glasgow Cross. He and Aggie had had a few brushes in the past. He took great pleasure in informing Aggie that after a recent plane ride to America, on a Corporation fact-finding mission, he had found that he couldn't get into his shoes.

Aggie's response was immediate. 'So yer feet swelled, tae!'

'I didn't come on this tram to be insulted, conductress!' he blustered.

'Oh, where dae ye normally go?'

❖ ❖

The drunk sat holding his precious bottle while talking incoherently to himself.

At the next stop a young woman got on, holding what appeared to be a newly born baby. She sat opposite the drunk and gave her baby a bottle of milk.

The drunk suddenly sat up. 'Aw the wee soul. Is it a new wean?' he asked.

Cautiously she answered, 'Aye, he's only two days old.'

'Right, ah'm gonnae open ma bottle an' we can aw wet the baby's heid.'

He then bawled out, 'Hey, onybuddy oan this caur got a screwtap opener?'

No one answered. He repeated his request. 'Onybuddy goat a screwtap opener so we can aw wet this wee wean's heid?'

Aggie had finished collecting fares on the upper deck, and when she came down onto the platform she demanded, 'Hey, who's wantin' a screwtap opener?'

'It's me. Ye know, tae wet this wee wean's heid.'

'That's awfa nice o' ye, sunshine, but by the looks o' ye you've already done it in advance.'

'Is that a wee insinuation, conductress?'

'Naw, a big wan. Can ye no' see the wean's already oan the bottle. Aff… o-f-f… aff!…'

❖ ❖

Some passengers were obviously going to the dog racing. The caur stopped and there was a man with three greyhounds waiting to board. Big Aggie immediately told him, 'Wan dug only oan each deck.'

'But Prancer here is the favourite tae win his race.'

'In that case he'll have nae bother prancin' tae the track.' And she rang the bell.

❖ ❖

The man looked up admiringly at Aggie, his eyes flashed, and he said pointedly, 'Single. Yoker.'

The reply was instant. 'Merrit. Gorbals!'

❖ ❖

The young woman, a regular on the number 9, gave her fare to Aggie.

'Fur heaven's sake, that's some hair-do ye've had,' commented Aggie.

'Well, it is a bit short,' she admitted.

'Did they gie ye a pair o' knickers wi' it?'

'A pair o' knickers?'

'Aye, well sumbuddy's obviously made a right erse o' it!'

❖ ❖

The somewhat rotund woman slowly got on the tram and sat down with a sigh.

Then she addressed Aggie. 'Dae ye know, conductress, ah goat on this caur yesterday. It wis full but three men stood to give me their seats.'

'An' did ye take them?'

Two ladies alighted from Aggie's tram. 'Did ye see that conductress on that number 9 tram?' one asked the other. 'Glared at me as if ah hudnae paid ma fare.'

'So whit did you dae?'

'Ah glared right back as if ah had.'

'So, did ye get away wi' it?'

'Ur you kidding. It wis that Big Aggie MacDonald. Came bouncing doon the caur and demanded ma money. A stoater, that yin.'

The young girl confided in Aggie.

'Aggie, it's terrible. Ah'm shocked. Ah couldna believe it. Ah caught ma boyfriend flirting.'

'Och, that's nothin' tae worry aboot. That's how ah caught wan o' mine tae, dearie.'

The woman had given Aggie hassle in the past. When Aggie came to take her money she looked up an' sneered, 'Aw, it's you, big yin.'

Aggie eyed her up an' down. 'Aye, it's me. Fur a minute ah didnae recognize you. It wis the most enjoyable minute ah've had a' day.'

'You're a right wan tae talk, so you are,' came the reply.

'Listen, hen. Ah'm no' going tae have a battle o' wits wi ye. Ah never attack onybuddy that's unarmed.'

❖ ❖

The well-dressed woman got on the tram in Argyle Street. 'I must say, conductress, I am not too keen oan yer uniform. Especially that hat. It's old fashioned so it is. See when I'm down in the dumps, I just get myself a new hat.'

Aggie glanced at the woman's hat. 'Listen, missus, ah'm in a good mood the day otherwise ah wid gie ye the obvious answer.'

❖ ❖

The smarmy young man was a regular passenger into town. He was forever telling Aggie about his exploits, and how wonderful he was. 'And ah've jist got masell a wee smasher o' a girlfriend. Last night she told me ah wis extremely handsome.'

'Ye must have been feedin' her guide dog, son.'

❖ ❖

On the lower deck saloon the posh gentleman in the bowler hat sat fiddling with his glasses, then asked, 'Excuse me, conductress, is this tramcar proceeding to Enniesland?'

'Naw,' replied Aggie. 'It's a number 9. So ectually, old chap, we is no' even meandering to Kailvinside.'

❖ ❖

'Wull ye no' be happy tae gie up the trams in September, Aggie,' asked the woman. 'Ah mean, yer getting' oan a bit, sure ye are?'

'Huh. Listen tae who's talking. Sumbuddy that probably sat behind Rabbie Burns at the school.'

❖ ❖

Aggie loved to gossip. One of her regulars pointed out to Aggie a young lady travelling on the caur. 'Look at the way yon is dressed. Her skirt is up tae her oxters. An' she's sittin there like a miserable lookin' scunner. Gie ye the boke jist tae look at her.'

'Aye,' replied Aggie. 'Her face is sour. If she put on face cream it wid curdle.'

'Sumbuddy wis tellin' me, Aggie, that she's good at languages. Apparently speaks six, and cannae say 'no' in any o' them. Dae you speak any languages, Aggie?'

'Jist Glaswegian. Ah'm quite fluent in that!'

❖ ❖

The teenager had given Aggie cheek in the past. He was forever blowing his trumpet.

'See when ah start tae work, ah'm gonnae start at the bottom,' he informed the conductress.

'Yer aimin' too high, sunshine.'

❖ ❖

The wee drunk was annoying Aggie with his stories. She had heard them many times. Finally he said,

'What would the world be like without a wee joke?'

'Fur a start you widnae be alive.'

❖ ❖

'Whit aboot that wee Inspector that you were always fightin' wi', Aggie? Is he still alive?'

'Aye. But if he had his life tae live ower again, he would still fall in love wi' himsell.'

❖ ❖

'Aggie, ah love yer patter,' said the passenger. 'An' you're aye busy aw day chattin' away as you go up an' doon the caur. Ur ye no' tired at the end o' the day?'

'Ah um. At the end o' ma shift ah can hardly keep ma mooth open.'

❖ ❖

'Aggie! Aggie! It's no fair,' exclaimed one of the regulars. 'See that big fat women there, well, when ah wis getting' oan she jumped the queue.'

'Don't worry, hen,' replied Aggie. 'Ah'll sort her out. Ah know that wummin. Mind ye, ah'm surprised she jumped the queue fur she's that thick she couldnae jump tae a conclusion!'

❖ ❖

The man was sitting on the top deck. 'Conductress, this is the rush hour an' we have been sittin' here for 15 minutes.'

'Well, it is Argyle Street at eight o'clock in the mornin' an it's busy. There are aboot ten caurs behind us an' another ten ahead o' us,' replied Aggie. 'But yer right. It is the rush hour. So if ah wis you ah wid rush doon the stairs, rush aff this caur, an' rush tae yer work.'

❖ ❖

'Conductress, let me ask you a question,' enquired the worried tourist. 'I have heard that sometimes this Glasgow of yours can be a very tough town. Is that right?'

'Naw, don't worry aboot goin' roon Glesca, missus,' replied Aggie. 'This is the friendliest, most helpful city in the hale world, so it is. Even if sumbuddy hits ye o'er the heid an' steals yer purse, they'll still gie ye directions how tae get ye tae the hospital.'

❖ ❖

Aggie was busy chatting.

'See her four seats up,' observed Aggie. 'She isnae whit ye wid call pretty, but she is nice.'

'Aye,' came the reply. 'She's really a fallen angel.'

'Pity she landed oan her face.'

❖ ❖

The young chap with the one leg boarded the tram and sat down just inside the caur. Aggie knew him well.

'So, where ur ye aff tae the night,' she asked.

'A'm away tae the dancin' at Barrowland. See if ah can get masel a lumber.'

'Good fur you. Mind, nae daein' the hokey cokey, noo.'

❖ ❖

It was a cold Saturday morning, and two nice wee boys sat on the lower deck wearing only shirts and shorts, though each held a jumper in their laps.

'It would freeze you ootside,' said Aggie. 'Get them jumpers oan ye, lads.'

'But wur gonnae use them fur a goalpost in the park, miss.'

'So where's yer ball?'

The boys looked at one other in dismay. 'Aw, naw. We forgot tae bring it!'

Aggie looked around. All the other passengers were

occupied. 'Listen, here's a shilling, boys. Dinny tell anybuddy, noo. Ye'll get wan in the shops next tae the park.' Then as she saw a passenger turning round to look, she shouted. 'An' get these bliddy jumpers oan right noo!'

Aggie then quietly whispered to the boys. 'You see, ah don't want anybuddy tae think ah'm getting' saft. Ah've goat ma reputation tae think o'.'

❖ ❖

'Aggie, some o' the trams are awfa slow. Nae wonder they're being phased oot.'

'Well, they've been aroon a long time,' countered Aggie. 'Probably thoosands o' years.'

'Aggie! Don't be daft. They've been in Glesca less than a hundred years.'

'Let me tell you, sunshine,' said Aggie, a smile lighting up her face. 'The Glesca caurs are even mentioned in the Guid Book.'

'Noo ye are kiddin' me.'

'Naw, naw. It says in the Guid Book that God created every creepin' thing!'

❖ ❖

Aggie was in a right old mood. 'Hey, you, mister, yer dug has fouled ma platform. Ye'll need tae clean it up.'

'Ah'll stick his nose in it an' he'll no' dae it again. But it's your job tae keep yer caur clean, conductress. This Corporation caur is fur the public's convenience.'

Aggie had him by the scruff of the neck in a minute. 'Listen you, smarty-pants. You clean it up right noo or ah'll stick your nose in it. You're a public inconvenience!'

The man cleaned it up.

As he got off at his stop he commented to Aggie. 'Ah'm reporting you tae the Corporation. It wis only a wee shit.'

'Aye, an' you're a bigger wan.'

Big Aggie's Memorable Last Day

In her wee room and kitchen Aggie didn't need an alarm to wake up on time in the morning. The one window faced east and only a net curtain graced the glass, so by 5.30 the light was already pouring in, even on cloudy days. On sunny days the sun shone through, highlighting the exhausted furniture. She lay in the darkness and sighed, then picked up her packet of cigarettes. Boy, she needed one.

It was the final day, Tuesday 4 September. The caurs had officially finished on Saturday but a souvenir service was being put on today. It would be a Coronation; some were still in reasonable condition. At least she was lucky to be conducting it.

The day she had dreaded had come at last. Aggie closed her eyes and tried to ignore the snores and grunts of her man, too deep in sleep to notice she was awake.

Finally Aggie dragged herself out of bed, yawned, and drew in an unhappy lungful of the smell of coal fires before starting her morning ritual of coughing. It was raining, again. 'Some weather for September,' she thought. Then she smiled as she remembered the depot party on Saturday in the canteen at the

Dalmarnock Depot. Everybody had been there, music blaring out and most of the staff a wee bit fu'.

Aggie had also been caught up in the euphoria, brought on by nostalgia, fears for the future and drink. In fact she could hardly remember the number of dances she had rocked and twisted to, although she had to acknowledge she did have to stop on a number of occasions to catch her breath. 'It's aw they 'gaspers' that cause it,' she mused as another fit of coughing overtook her.

And sure enough the wee man himself, Inspector Campbell, had been there, looking something of a wallflower as he stood alone drinking Irn-Bru. Perhaps it had been the influence of a few jars, or the fact that she had recently jested with Campbell she would dance with him, that made Aggie wander over to join him.

'Ur ye no' dancin', Inspector?'

'No, Mrs MacDonald.'

'So is that you finished wi' the trams, then. Ur ye transferrin' on tae the buses or trolley-buses?'

'No, Mrs MacDonald. I am hoping to take up a position within Glasgow Corporation that requires my dedication and skills.'

'Well, everybuddy knows ye've goat dedication in spades, but where's the skills? Onybuddy could check a tram ticket an' tell a driver he's five minutes late.'

'Mrs MacDonald, as you will know I was always very

precise with my observations. I have stuck to the rules through thick and thin, unlike some I could mention.'

'Well, why don't ye put yer rule book away fur the night an' we'll hae a wee twist oan the flair. Eh? Whit dae ye say?'

'Do you really think I would do one of those modern so-called dances? I am a quickstep man. Anyway, I am not sure I could dance with you, Mrs MacDonald, given the high position I have attained in Glasgow Corporation.'

'High position!' Aggie suddenly lost it, mad at herself for having felt sorry for the wee creep. 'Listen, yer five feet nothin' wi' yer bunnet oan. This wis yer last chance tae show everybuddy that yer human.'

'Mrs MacDonald, I have my own standards to hold onto. Can you not tell that by the determined look on my face?'

'Yer face! Let me tell you, sunshine, that your face reminds me o' a wet weekend in Girvan! And see that wee rulebook and timetable, ye can finally stick them up yer erse!'

Aggie heard convulsions of stifled laughter from those around as she flounced over to Jimmy Tamson. Soon the pair were twisting the night away.

Aye, it had been a wonderful party. She could hardly remember how she got home. But now the reality of the situation was upon her. The final hours. Aggie dressed slowly, ready for her duties later on in the day. As her

60th birthday was only two days off, and as she was the longest serving conductress on the trams, she had been chosen to be the conductress on the very last tram in the Tramway System. It was to run to Auchenshuggle, leaving Anderston Cross at 5pm.

In the evening a tram procession of 20 caurs would take place. On one of the trams would be Lord Provost, Jean Roberts, plus all the city dignitaries including Mr ERL Fitzpayne, the boss of the transport system. Aggie and all her mates had arranged they would stand and cheer, perhaps even have a wee greet, as the auld caurs of yesteryear went by.

Aggie spent the day in a mournful mood. Couldn't settle to do anything and husband Tommy quickly discovered he couldn't do anything right. She was on the count down to the evening's run on the last scheduled caur.

After what had seemed like a very long day, finally, just before five o'clock, Aggie arrived at Anderston Cross. There it stood; the last tram to Auchenshuggle. She stood for a minute looking at the sight of the ill-fated Coronation number 1174 with its green, cream and orange livery. It had clearly fallen on hard times, its lines dulled by age with faded and scratched paint-work. It stood on its elderly joints with unsightly black blobs around the wheels. Aggie swallowed hard. *Her* trams were about to disappear for ever.

A large queue had formed, all anxious to join this special tram to Auchenshuggle and purchase the souvenir ticket especially printed for the occasion. At five o'clock, with a full tram and a heavy heart, Aggie rang the bell, and off they set.

All the passengers were feeling sentimental though a few were surprised at the raised cost of sixpence for the pink souvenir ticket. 'Ur they no' a bit dear, Aggie,' a few people had commented.

'A sad, sad day for Glasgow. No more of our lovely trams,' a tram buff said to Aggie as she gave him his ticket.

'Aye, right enough it's awfa sad,' Aggie agreed. 'Ah never thought ah'd say it, but ah jist wish a cheeky wummin wi' a face like a skelpit erse an' half a dozen weans plus a dug that peed oan the flair, wid come oan. It wid bring back a few memories an' maybe cheer me up.'

'Aye, well, never mind, here's Auchenshuggle coming up, Aggie. Ye can have a last shot o' changin' the screen, seats an' bow collector. Take yer mind aff the situation. Bye the way, are you going to go onto the buses, noo?'

'Naw, everybuddy asks me that. Ah'm too auld, noo. Nearly 60 ye know. So ah'll jist call it a day. Retire tae ma villa in the South o' France,' she chuckled.

When the tram stopped at the Auchenshuggle crossover Aggie looked out at the weather. The rain, which until a few minutes earlier had been pattering globes of water on dirty puddles, was thankfully starting to ease off. It looked as though the sun might actually shine. There were ten minutes before they were due to return so some of the passengers had got out and were milling around the tram.

'It's been a right dreich Glesca day, the day. It wid be nice if it wid dry up fur a while,' Aggie thought miserably. She sat on a seat, took out her fags and lit up. Her mind went back through the years. Aye, it had been fun on the caurs. The trams had always played a major part in her life. They seemed to have been in Glasgow for ever. In fact she had met all of her three husbands on the caurs.

It was amazing how time had passed so quickly. She had joined the transport system in 1941, during the war. Many men had gone off to fight and women were being drafted in to replace them both as drivers and conductresses. Being a social animal Aggie had opted for life as a conductress. Mind you, at that stage in her life she hadn't quite appreciated some of the characters she would meet up with on the caurs. Aggie chuckled. She really had enjoyed all her years. All the nonsense, fun and challenges.

She remembered one particular evening during the war. It was a night, when in spite of rationing on coal supplies, acrid smog had blanketed the city. Blackout restrictions had also applied. She remembered her tram crawling up Union Street, fog seeping into the lower deck, passengers coughing, while the driver operated the warning bell as he drove in almost complete darkness.

At a caur stop, though heaven alone knows how the driver could have seen it, an entire band had materialised out of the throat-catching yellow fog. Some had trudged upstairs, others sat throughout the lower saloon deck.

The next thing Aggie was aware of was that the tram had filled with 'Chattanooga Choo Choo', the

Glenn Miller favourite. 'Ah bet it went faster than we're goin' the night,' she had thought.

The auld Standard then crept through the fog round to St Vincent Street, before turning into Hope Street. The profusion of music continued, cheering up the war-weary passengers on this dreadful night. Everyone's feet were tapping though the noise was completely lost against the music.

The caur continued its slow but noisy progress along the street, seemingly enveloped in a bubble of freezing, murky gloom. Aggie had gone round collecting fares, though conversation had been difficult. When she approached a saxophonist, who turned out to be the leader and conductor of the band, he put down his instrument. Raising his voice he explained, 'You see, conductress, we're going to give a concert tonight, that is if the audience actually turn up with this awful weather. We haven't been able to get together to practise because of the blackout, so we thought we'd do it on your tram. I trust that is all right?'

'Nae bother,' Aggie had replied. 'In fact ah should really charge the other passengers extra fur the entertainment. Mind you, it's gey funny fur me being the conductress collectin' fares fae you... a conductor, tae.'

The conductor smiled, and signalled to the players in his immediate vicinity to move on to another piece. The smooth music continued with the haunting mellow strain of 'In the Mood', and it was exactly then that she became aware of the drummer. He was really into the wonderful enticing style of Miller's music. When he saw her he had smiled over his drum and winked.

'Mmmm. No' bad lookin',' she had thought. The guy had been a fast worker. He had arranged a date with Aggie to go dancing at the Locarno the following week. In six months they were married. 'Whit a big mistake that wis,' Aggie thought. 'A big chancer if ever there wis wan. Oot most nights playing wi' the band then comin' in drunk. Then there had been the time when two lassies came to the door claiming he had fathered their weans. Then the ever increasing pile of bills.'

So after a few months she had just told him to take his drum and beat it!

It had also been that very night with the band on board that Aggie first come across another nuisance in her life. The caur had just shivered to a halt when a small and lean young fellow, with thin lips and a perm-anent smirk to match, smartly dressed in the uniform of Glasgow Transport, had stepped out of the swirling smog.

'I'm Inspector Campbell,' he had announced. 'Why is there such a racket on this tramcar, conductress?'

'It's no' a racket, Inspector. It's Glenn Miller favourites,' Aggie replied, immediately sizing him up. 'It's jist a pity ah hudnae sized up that big chancer ah married,' she thought.

'Why are you as an employee of the transport system allowing these individuals to make this awful noise? There appears to be other passengers on board. You must think of all our travelling public, conductress.'

'Everybuddy is enjoying it, Inspector. It's wartime. We aw need a wee bit cheerin' up.'

'I agree, conductress, but we have a strict blackout. This noise could alert enemy planes.'

'Cummoan, Inspector! Ye've goat tae be at the kiddin'. How could a wee band like this possibly alert the Luftwaffe?'

'Well, erm, anyway, I do not like it. Please have them desist, conductress.'

Aggie had stood enough. 'Desist! Whit school did you go tae, wee man?'

'Conductress,' he said sternly. 'I am an Inspector. You are merely a conductress. So I expect nothing less than courtesy and respect.'

'Aye, right, Inspector.' But under her breath murmured, 'We've goat a right pipsqueak here. But ah better watch whit ah say. Ah need tae keep ma job.'

'Okay, Inspector, ah'll away an' talk tae MacNamara, the leader o' this band, and get him tae stoap.'

Upon being told they would have to 'desist' playing, the leader stood, waved his arms and soon most of the tram was quiet. A quick shuffle upstairs and all music stopped.

'That's the way I like my trams, conductress,' snorted the Inspector.

'Dae ye no' like music, then, Inspector,' Aggie had asked.

'I will have you know that I am competent on a number of instruments. My beloved mother sent me for piano and trumpet lessons,' he announced proudly.

'Is that right, Inspector. I bet ye cannae remember how tae play ony o' them noo?'

Pointing to a young man holding a trumpet, Campbell said. 'I could give you a quick example of my prowess, conductress. The 'Trumpet Voluntary' in D Major.'

Aggie grabbed the musician's trumpet and smiled, 'Right, gie us a blaw, then.'

To everyone's astonishment the music produced by the Inspector was clear and tuneful. As Aggie had said later, 'His mother would have been proud o' him.'

When he was finished the passengers, including the band, all applauded. Campbell's face was triumphant, an absolute picture of delight. He even took a few bows before stepping off into the blanket of fog.

'That was a big surprise, conductress,' MacNamarra

had observed. 'One minute your Inspector was complaining about the noise then he surprises us all with a solo. He could join our group anytime.'

'Yer right,' admitted Aggie. 'An' naebuddy dropped a bomb, either. But ah can see ah'm gonnae have problems wi' that yin, even if he is guid at blowin' his ain trumpet!'

Then Aggie's memory jumped to an occasion just before Christmas one year. Snow had fallen a few days earlier and was again floating down in large snowflakes driven on by a cold easterly wind. The old snow and slush were now completely covered in a new winter wonderland. Soon it would be a complete whiteout.

The Standard tram was lost in its cover of white. Aggie had been up top twice, lowering the window above the destination box and quickly wiping off the sticking snow from the glass. At the same time Aggie was blasted with a white torrent of snow. Once she finally got the window back up she gave herself a quick jiggle to shake off the clinging flakes, and rubbed her hands together. It was freezing.

The tram had come to a halt. People sheltering in shopdoors and tenement closes trudged over to the caur, all keen to climb aboard to get out of the weather. They surged onto the platform, stamping off the snow sticking to their footwear in the process. Aggie eventually managed to get everyone on board, before noticing that one of the boarding passengers was dressed in a Santa Claus outfit.

Inside it was somewhat warmer though wind still whistled through from the platform. Aggie was happy to move up the shoogling tram away from the cold wind. 'Ferrs, pal-eeze,' she shouted, coppers jingling in her huge hand.

She had collected various fares before she came face to face with the man who would ultimately be spouse number two; Santa Claus himself.

'Right, Santa,' Aggie had smiled. 'Where ur ye goin'... wonderland or doon chimneys?'

'Lewis's in Argyle Street.'

'Ur you their Santa this year?'

'Well, wan o' them. There's actually three, ye see. We take turns.'

'So, if ah wis tae go tae Lewis's an' sit oan yer knee what would ah get fae Santa?'

'Listen, if you sat oan ma knee ah know whit ah wid get. A broken leg,' he grinned.

'Ya cheeky bugger,' replied Aggie. But she liked his style.

'Well, ah might gie ye a wee cheeper, too,' he smiled.

'Santa had travelled on her caur a number of times during the run-up to Christmas and in that time a friendship developed. Soon they were 'walking out' together, and a few months later Bert, aka Santa, had asked if she would like to become his 'Mrs Claus'?

Aggie had been undecided. She had made a mistake with the drummer. Another thing was they wouldn't have anywhere to live, and Bert didn't seem to have any regular job apart from his yearly one at Lewis's, so they would be dependent on her conductress's wages.

By now Bert had met her parents a few times. He lived with his sister as their parents had passed on, so he suggested they stay with her until they found a place of their own.

If she had met his sister before or at the wedding she would have known what he was really like, and would never have contemplated marriage.

After a quiet marriage ceremony there was no honeymoon. Just a few drinks in a pub. Then Aggie plus her suitcase moved in with his sister.

Later that night she moved out. His 'sister' was his long time 'bidie-in', and Bert had shown Aggie the bed where all three of them would sleep.

Aggie then found out that this particular Santa was nothing but a Christmas cracker. She also heard later that he was a serial canoodler with a succession of little dears continually sitting on Santa's knee.

So Santa was dispatched to join the drummer, and Aggie determined to be much more careful of her choice of men in future.

Then a few years later came mild-mannered Tommy. He was a regular passenger on her caur who always sat

LAST TRAM TAE AUCHENSHUGGLE!

quietly on the upper deck enjoying a fag while reading his newspaper. Occasionally, of an evening, and with a wee dram in him he would exchange pleasantaries with Aggie. 'Nice man,' she had concluded.

What brought them together was an incident on Aggie's tram a few months later. Aggie had heard shouting upstairs and dashed up to see what the kerfuffle was all about. A hard-faced, Glesca keelie with an intimidating look was standing over a white-faced Tommy. 'Ye did it oan purpose, wee man, ah'm gonnae huv you. Rip yer face open fae end tae end wi' this!' A half-open razor flashed in his hand. Purposefully he extended it.

'Hey,' shouted Aggie. 'Whit's aw this nonsense aboot? This is diabolical!'

The tough snarled. 'Listen, hen. Take ma advice. Jist you go doon the sterrs an' collect ferrs or ah'll start oan you next, wance ah've re-arranged this fella's face. He deliberately tripped me as ah passed.'

'Ah did not. He kicked ma foot on purpose,' Tommy pleaded.

Aggie turned to a respectable looking gent sitting nearby. 'Here you, haud ontae these,' and she slung her cash bag and ticket machine off her enormous bosom onto his lap. Aggie clenched her jaw muscles and moved up to stand directly in front of the hard man, brought her face close to his and stared into his cold eyes.

'So, big man, ah've goat tae say you've really got balls pickin' a fight wi' this innocent wee fella,' Aggie snapped sarcastically.

'Aye, hen. Ah've mair balls than you'll ever have!'

Aggie's massive hand moved like lightening. In a flash she had his 'crown jewels' clenched in her fist. She squeezed hard. The razor dropped and a desperate squealing noise was heard.

'Aye, yer right,' agreed Aggie. 'Ye dae hae balls. But ah'm gonnae rip them aff ye right noo, ya numpty.'

An almost silent pleading of 'Nawwwwwwwwwww. Aaaaaaaaaaaa.' clearly carried throughout the top deck.

By this time the tram had come to a halt. No one moved. Everyone looked on mesmerised as Aggie tightened her grip.

'Will ah get the polis?' asked a passenger.

'Naw, an ambulance,' retorted Aggie.

Still with a firm grip on the man's 'crown jewels', Aggie and the hard man slowly descended the stairs, Aggie going down backwards. On the platform she stopped, propelled him round, went eyeball to eyeball and growled. 'Sunshine, this is your lucky day. Ah'm gonnae let ye keep yer balls but ah don't think they're gonnae be much good tae ye fur a while. If ah ever see you oan this tram again ah'll wear them fur earrings!' A massive foot was lifted and the toe of her shoe replaced her tight fist. The yelp was blood-curdling. Aggie shoved him off and he toppled backwards on to the cobbles.

Applause rang out thoughout the caur. Aggie calmly turned, climbed the stairs, recovered her cash bag and ticket machine, then rang the bell.

Off trundled the tram, the passengers agog at what they had just witnessed.

As Aggie once again started collecting fares she couldn't help but overhear a couple of shipyard workers talking, 'Believe me, tae get the better o' that conductress

ye wid need a rivet gun, two fore-
men and a hale squad o' platers.'
Aggie had liked that.

A few stops later on, a shaking
Tommy had come down from
the top deck. He briefly thanked
Aggie and quickly got off. But the
following day he was back, a
bunch of flowers for Aggie in his
arms. Aggie had gone weak at the
knees. It had been a while since a
man had given her roses. Their
friendship had then grown over some months of his
regular travelling on her caur. However it had taken
the bold Aggie to suggest they finally go out together.
In fact, if she remembered correctly, she was the one
who had proposed marriage. Anyway, it had gone well.
They were still married, had three of a family, although
sometimes Tommy did have a wee bit ower much to
drink. Still, he was a good man.

And then there was Hogmany. Hogmanay was a
funny old day on the trams. From early morning
housewives were out and about buying the traditional
fundamentals for Scottish life on 31 December.

On the trams their shopping bags bulged with boiled
hams, black puddings, sausages, ashet pies, steak pies,
cherry cake, sultana cake and black bun. Perhaps even

ginger and blackcurrant cordial essence. Clootie
dumpling, trifles, shortbread and tablet would have
been made at home some days before the great event.

Queues stretched out on to pavements throughout
the city from licensed grocers as folks stocked up for
the night ahead with their favourite tipples.

Once housewives got home, it was on with their
peenies, then cleaning and scrubbing the house ready
for the New Year.

Menfolk would work at least part of the day,
perhaps have a pint going home, just to be in the mood
for the forthcoming proceedings.

In the hours before midnight it was relatively quiet
on the trams, most people at home finishing their
preparations, listening to the wireless or watching
television. Then all outside doors would be opened for
the five minutes before 12 o'clock to let the old year
out and the new one in, although some Glaswegians
still opted to congregate at the Trongate to welcome
in the New Year.

Once midnight came, folks would set off on their
rounds of first-footing with neighbours, relatives and
friends. Every house had its lights on and the sound
of laughter, 'Happy New Year!' and 'Slainte!' filled the
air. Perhaps a piper or an accordionist would open
their windows and greet the world with 'A Guid New
Year Tae Yin an' Aw'.

For some reason **Aggie MacDonald** had usually found herself on the last shift at **Hogmanay**. 'At least you didn't normally get aggressive drunks on board at **Hogmanay**,' she mused. More often it was slightly inebriated men and women with sentimental tears in their eyes who, after the 'Bells', kissed, hugged and slobbered over each other, including Aggie, and who insisted that everyone share their New Year bottle. It was amazing how in Glasgow strangers became instant friends with smiles and greetings all round of 'awrrabest!'

Aggie remembered once on the top deck at Hogmanay, under the mellow caur lighting, a young couple snuggled up together, swaying against each other with the motions of the tramcar. As Aggie gave them their tickets the young man had run his finger down the window showing the ever-forming condensation, and observed, 'The windaes up here are aw steamed up.'

'Aye, so they ur,' Aggie had agreed. 'An' by the looks o' you two, so are youse.'

The girl blushed, looked up and said, 'Ye see we're away hame tae ask ma feyther if we can get merrit.'

'Aw, that's awfa nice, hen,' Aggie had replied. 'Ah hope it aw turns oot well fur ye.'

The following week the young lady had boarded Aggie's tram, proudly showing off a sparkling engagement ring.

And then there had been the handsome big fella in the old trench coat, sitting smoking on the top deck, definitely well into the spirit of Hogmanay. Aggie had noticed huge bulges under his coat. She asked cautiously 'Is that yer bottles aw ready fur first-footin', then?'

'Well, sort o',' came the reply. He unfastened his belt, undid the buttons on the trench coat and removed coal briquettes. 'Ye see,' he explained, 'ah've goat four o' them. They're fur ma four girlfriends. They don't know each other so ah've goat tae first foot them individually. Ah'm a coalman an' a goat friendly wi' they four lassies oan ma rounds.'

'Good heavens, you're a right Romeo!'

'So ah am,' he agreed with a wink. 'The problem is ah love them aw.' He pointed unsteadily towards the briquettes. 'This wan's fur Molly, this wan fur Agnes, this wan fur Myra, an this wan fur Jenny.' Then he staggered to his feet. 'This is ma first stoap,' he slurred. 'Ah'm awa tae see ma wee Molly.'

At the top of the stairs he stopped, blew Aggie a kiss, then stood on his trench coat belt and took a flying header down the stairs, his tackety boots occasionally making contact with the tram walls before he landed in a heap on the platform below.

Aggie was quick to descend the stair only to find that the big fella seemed to have survived unscathed though he was now covered in coal dust. He got to his feet and felt in his large pockets for his briquettes. Only one had survived the fall. He held it up to Aggie, smiled sadly from his now coal black face and said, 'Well, it looks as though only wan o' ma lady freens is gonnae see me the night.' So saying he stepped off the platform, mistimed his step, and the remaining briquette in his hand broke into smithereens.

Once more he got up, turned and grinned at Aggie. 'Onyway, hen. Happy New Year. Awrrabest tae you an' yours.'

'And you, sunshine,' said Aggie before she rang the bell. 'Some first-foot yon. Aw he seems tae dae is fall ower his ain feet,' she thought, 'och, well. He is tall, quite handsome and noo he is definitely dark.'

It was almost one o'clock in the morning as the now empty tram was shoogling its way back to the depot, that a small uniformed figure had appeared at the side of the street and raised an arm.

'Aw, naw, it's that wee numpty Campbell,' muttered Aggie. 'That wan wid gie ye enough headaches fur half a dozen Askit powders. Looks as though ah've another firstfoot, only this wan is wee, pink an' plain as purridge.'

Inspector Campbell it was, who immediately complained that the tram was filthy with coal dust. Aggie had to tell him about the episode with the romantic coal man. 'Anyway,' she reassured Campbell, 'the cleaners will soon clean it up at the depot. Ah must say that ah'm surprised yer still oan duty at this time in the mornin', Inspector.'

'Mrs MacDonald, if the trams are running, then I always consider myself to be on duty.'

'So is that you away hame noo tae indulge yersell in shortbread an' Co-operative ginger wine essence?'

'Now, Mrs MacDonald,' he cautioned. 'I think you are being somewhat forward. Indeed I have come to the conclusion that somehow you would be pleased to see the back of me. In fact I would probably go so far as to say that you wish I would pass on during this New Year so you could come and urinate on my grave.'

'Inspector Campbell!' exclaimed Aggie, somewhat taken aback at this bold statement. 'Let me tell you that although ah deal wi' them everyday... ah personally hate queues!'

Glasgow Uni rag days had been challenging, too. Students were allowed to travel free but were supposed to get off once they had completed their collection. 'Goad help us,' thought Aggie. 'Ah can remember aw that mayhem well.'

There had been the young fellow dressed as a pirate, his face blackened with cocoa powder and Nivea cream,

who had tried to take Aggie's money bag and ticket
machine so he could go around the tram collecting fares
while at the same time getting his can filled. He wouldn't
take 'no' for an answer so she threw him off at the
next stop. The 'pirate' then jumped in beside the driver
and tried to persuade him to let him drive. Aggie only
realised this when the tram stopped abruptly and the
student flew off onto the road.

Aggie remembered the young student dressed as a
robot who had gone around the passengers jingling a
bucket to which a notice was attached: 'MAK MA
BUCKET FU'. It had been with great difficulty that
Aggie had managed to restrain a grateful drunk from
doing just that.

A kilted student dressed as Bonnie Prince Charlie
had had a sign around his neck which read, 'SEE MY
BUM FOR A SHILLING!' He had smiled at Aggie and
asked, 'Listen, conductress. Do you fancy a wee decko
at my posterior?'

'Naw, son. Ah've had mair bums oan this tram than
ah could count.' But she still gave him a donation.

Most of the tram passengers tolerated the nonsense
and were mildly amused, although some were clearly
embarrassed. Aggie secretly enjoyed it although she
would stand no nonsense.

But Aggie would forever remember one wee lad,
obviously fortified with a pint or two, who had caused

chaos. He had changed the destination screen and then tugged on the rope for the bow collector which caused the lights in the tram to flicker. The student then ran wildly up and down the aisles with a flour bomb in his hand, threatening to toss it into the lower deck if passengers didn't put money into his collecting can.

'Right, sunshine, that's enough!' shouted Aggie. She grabbed him by the ear and looked into his wild eyes. 'Whit's yer name, sunshine?'

'Humphry,' he squealed.

'Humphry! Whit kind o' name is that fur a Scotsman?'

'I'm English.'

'Then whit ur ye dae'n at Glesca Uni, Humph?'

'I'm studying English.'

'Well, you watch ma lips, cause you're really gettin' up ma humph, Humph. Ah'm no' gonnae speak tae ye in English cause ah only speak fluent Glesca. Listen, son, you is gonnae add up tae nuthin in life wi' aw yer kerry oan. Absolute zilch. Yer o'er the top, Humph. Dae ye hear me?'

It pained Humphry to nod but he just managed it.

'Ah didnae go tae the Uni, Humph. You're lucky. But if you don't calm doon an' sober up then you're just gonnae be a waste o' space. Naebuddy but naebuddy is gonnae flour bomb ma tram! Ah kick the erse o' eejits like you aff this tram every other day.'

Still holding his red, now somethat enlarged ear,

she led him to the edge of the auld Standard's platform. 'Have a wee sample, Humph.' Humphry yelped as a foot connected with his rear end.

'Whit a wally,' Aggie had thought.

It had been around ten years later that Aggie received a shock. She was told by the depot manager that Mr ERL Fitzpayne, the overall god of the transport system, wanted to see her.

'They're oot tae make an example o' me,' she had thought. 'That wee toerag Campbell wull be behind this. Ah'll swing fur him yet, so ah will.'

The meeting was the following day at two o'clock at Fitzpayne's office at 46 Bath Street. By midday an extremely anxious Aggie had gone through a couple of packets of fags.

However in Fitzpayne's office she was surprised to find two very relaxed people, both with their jackets off.

Fitzpayne himself sat back in a leather swivel chair with elbows winged up in the air and his fingers interlaced behind his neck.

He smiled as Aggie entered. 'In you come, Agnes, I have an admirer of yours here to say hello.'

'Jings,' Aggie had thought, 'there cannae be mony o' them in a pound.'

The other man rose with a smile and took Aggie's hand. For once she was totally confused. Her brain searched for a solution.

Fitzpayne said, 'Let me introduce you, Agnes, to Humphry Percival-Smyth, who is head of one of Britain's top companies.'

It still hadn't rung a bell with Aggie.

Humphry grinned and spoke in a Home Counties accent. 'Yes, you're definitely the lady I remember. Let me properly introduce myself. I'm the 'waste of space' whose 'erse' you kicked on a uni rag day many years ago.'

'I don't think I want to hear this,' said Fitzpayne with a chuckle.

Suddenly it dawned on Aggie. 'Aw, Humph! Noo ah remember you. You've brushed up well, son, err, sur.'

'I certainly have, and it's all because of you, Agnes. Our little incident has remained firmly in my mind over all the years. You have been my inspiration.' He kissed her cheek and turned round to produce a massive box of chocolates which he placed in Aggie's unbelieving

hands. 'I will always be extremely grateful for your wise words and actions, though my rear end has never quite recovered,' he added with a smile.

A stunned, blushing Aggie just stood until she heard Fitzpayne say, 'Thank you, Agnes, that will be all. You may return to your duties now.'

Aggie, still agog, turned to take her leave. As she closed the office door her old confidence returned. She turned and said, 'Aye, an' if you don't keep at it, Humph, ah'll boot yer erse again!'

As the door finally closed she heard Humphry Percival-Smyth observe, 'Salt of the earth, that lady.'

As Aggie remembered that day, she thought, 'Aye, it wis nice tae be appreciated noo' an' again. Ah've been quite fortunate really, o'er aw the years.'

Big Aggie sat up with a start, jolted from her memories by the noises around her. It was time for the return trip from Auchenshuggle to the depot, and more passengers had squeezed on board the already crowded caur.

Soon the tram was again festooned in a profusion of noise. Everybody had excited faces, greeting Aggie with their cheerful patter. As the rain had temporarily stopped, some had taken photographs outside beside the faithful old beast. Then, with everyone inside they had set off for the short journey to Bridgeton Cross and the depot.

Some folks had brought along bottles of various beverages which they now sat sipping. There was also a cake shaped like a tram already sliced for distribution. Passengers joked, laughed and swapped tales of tram journeys of yesteryear as the old tram hummed along, blissfully unaware of its destiny.

Finally, as the Coronation neared the Dalmarnock Depot someone shouted for Aggie to make a speech. Suddenly her mouth went dry, a tear trickled down a cheek, but she managed to get out a few words.

'Right, youse... CUMMOANANGETAFF!'

Big Aggie's Tramlines

'Ye know, conductress, ma uncle used tae drive the trams, but he got sacked for careless driving.'

'Wis he tryin' tae overtake?'

❖ ❖

The young mother was sitting cuddling her newborn baby boy. The baby was smiling and making various gurgling and squealing noises.

'Aw, whit a lovely wee babe. A right wee smasher, so he is,' observed Aggie.

'He really is a good wee soul,' said the mother. 'Talks aw the time. Ah wonder whit he will dae when he's a man?'

'Well, aw they noises sound interesting an' mean absolutely nothing tae me, so he'll definitely be a Glesca cooncillor.'

❖ ❖

Inspector Campbell jumped on the caur and immediately challenged Aggie as to why she was hatless.

'Mrs MacDonald, I am shocked. Surely you know the regulation that all hats must be worn?'

'Ma hat is worn, Inspector. The bleedin' thing is threadbare.'

❖ ❖

Aggie was having difficulty in collecting fares as a drunk was pestering other passengers for money.

'Nae beggin' oan ma tram. Jist sit there an' be quiet,' Aggie told him.

'Listen! A've only wan leg missus, an' ah'm short o' a couple o' bob.'

'Jist because ye've wan leg doesnae mean ye can annoy decent travelling folks on ma tram.'

'Oh, it's your tram, is it?'

'Aye, an' ye'r aff at the next stop. Aff. O-F-F! Hop it!'

❖ ❖

The middle-aged woman was looking Aggie up and down. 'Ah've got tae say, conductress, that's an awful lookin' uniform the Corporation gie ye.'

'Well,' said Aggie politely. 'That's a nice dress you're wearin', missus, but who went fur the fittin' fur ye?'

The young woman was taking her time getting off the tram.

'Hurry up you,' said Aggie. 'Get aff quick. There are thoosands waitin' tae get oan this caur.'

'Ah'll dae it in ma ain guid time, conductress!'

'Get a move on or ah'll need tae gie ye a shove.'

'Listen. Have ye never heard that ye cannae shove yer granny aff a bus?' came the irritable reply.

'Heard it? Ah'm the wummin that pushes them aff. An' anither thing. Ye'r no' a granny, ye'r certainly no' ma granny... and this is no' a bus!'

Two passengers on Aggie's tram were discussing her. 'See that Big Aggie MacDonald, I bet ye every morning she brushes her teeth and sharpens her tongue. Here she comes noo. No doubt she'll make some sort of observation tae us the day.'

'You both had yer hair done, then?' asked Aggie as she gave them their tickets.

'No, conductress. I'll have you know we've both been at the beauticians today.'

'Aye, well, ye could maybe get them under the Trades Description Act.'

❖ ❖

The women was clearly agitated. 'Can this caur no' go a bit quicker?' she asked Aggie.

'Naw really,' replied Aggie. 'Whit's yer hurry?'

'Ah'm awa tae the doctor. Ah don't like the look o' ma man.'

'Well, ah better come wi' ye. Sometimes ah canny stand mine, either.'

'Ur ye serious that ye cannae stand him'

'Aye. Ah only married him because ah had a condition.'

'Whit wis it?'

'Pregnancy.'

❖ ❖

'Is this tram up tae time, conductress?'

'Wi' the driver I've goat the day you should jist be happy it's oan the rails.'

❖ ❖

The young policeman was irate. Aggie's tram had come off the rails at the points on a tight turn.

'The problem is,' explained Aggie, 'these Coronation caurs are prone tae this sort o' thing goin' roon bends.'

'But are there no' arrows tae warn yer driver?' asked the policeman.

'Him! Arrows! He widnae even see the Indians.'

❖ ❖

'Dae ye no' think that the sound o' the wheels on the rails is kind o' musical, you know, relaxing, conductress?' asked the elderly lady.

'Ah'm afraid ah huvnae a musical ear, dearie,' replied Aggie.

'Can ye no' play a musical instrument like a piano, then?'

'Believe me, dearie, ah wid have given ma right arm tae be a pianist.'

❖ ❖

The pretty young lady was a regular passenger. She always confided in Aggie, updating her on her various romances.

'So how's yer love life, hen?' asked Aggie.

'Oh, ah've got a new boyfriend. Ah met him at the weekend. He's very tall, quite good looking, and he's got big hands and big feet, and you know what that means,' she said with a smile.

'Aye,' said Aggie. 'Big gloves an' big socks.'

❖ ❖

As the small boy boarded the tram he slipped.
The penny he had been holding rolled off the edge
of the platform and down a drain. The wee lad burst
into tears.

Aggie looked at the tear-stained cheeks and told him,
'Och well, yer no' awfa big, so you'll no' take up much
room. In ye go an' sit doon, son.'

❖ ❖

The old Coronation was going fast, screaming round
curves. Many of the customers were clearly worried;
one woman let out a scream.

'Can ye no' dae something aboot yer driver, Aggie.
This caur is fair jumpin' aboot. This is murder polis!'

'We're a bit behind the day,' admitted Aggie. 'An' ma
driver is 'Larry the Lurch' the day, so jist dae whit he
does. When we go roon a bend he shuts his eyes.'

❖ ❖

Aggie unfortunately had a propensity to pass wind.
One day as she was taking the fares of a man and his
wife, Aggie just couldn't help herself.

The man was indignant. In a 'pan loaf' voice he said,
'How rude of you to belch in front of my wife!'

'Sorry, mister,' replied Aggie. 'Ah didnae know it wis
her turn.'

❖ ❖

Big Aggie was busy collecting fares when she came on an old neighbour. 'Hullowrerr, Gracie. Ye look as though ye'r in a dwam. Where ur ye goin'?'

'Hame tae die.'

'Whit! Ur ye ill?'

'No' jist noo, Aggie. But ah'm 63 the day. Ye see ma mither, feyther, three sisters an' ma granny aw died when they wur 63. So ah'm goin' hame tae die in the comfort o' ma ain bed. Ma number's jist aboot up.'

'But Gracie, dae ye no' know it'll cost nearly four hunderd pounds just tae bury ye.'

'But, Aggie, ah huvnae goat that kind o' money.'

'Well, if ah wis you, Gracie, ah widnae bother goin' tae ma bed when ye get hame. Go tae the bingo instead. Then if yer number does come up ye might win enough money fur yer funeral.'

The following week Gracie again boarded Aggie's tram.

'Ah see yer no' deid yet,' observed Aggie.

'Ah'm still here aw right, Aggie. Remember ye told me tae go tae the bingo? Well the 'snowball' came up an' ah wun a hunner pounds. Then on the way hame ah met ma brother. He telt me it wisna 63 when they aw died. It wis 73.'

'Great,' said Aggie. 'Noo ye've ten years tae save up the other three hunner fur yer funeral!'

❖ ❖

'Hey, conductress, what have we stopped for? Ah'm late for business,' complained a wee man in a bowler hat. 'And your driver now seems to be out with a bucket and is throwing something on the rails.'

'He's pittin' sand oan the rails so we get over this tricky wee gradient,' explained Aggie. 'Did ye think he wis going tae make, sand pies?'

❖ ❖

It was the terminus at Auchenshuggle and Aggie was having a sneaky fag. Two wee boys scampered up the stairs. Aggie heard a succession of clinks followed by laughter as they pushed over the back rests ready for the return journey.

When they clattered down the stairs, they shouted, 'That's yer top deck fixed, missus. Yer a bit fat tae be climbing stairs.'

'Ah'll tell ye whit ah'm good at lads... bootin' erses!' The two boys jumped off the tram still laughing.

Later as the tram moved back along its route, a passenger pointed out to Aggie that two tin cans were merrily bouncing along behind, tied to the tram with string.

'See if ah get ma haunds on these cheeky wee buggers,' Aggie said to herself. Then she thought, 'Och, ah wis the same at their age. In fact, ah huvnae changed... ' and she laughed.

❖ ❖

Big Aggie Moves
tae Auchenshuggle

'Ye see, Maisie,' Big Aggie confided to her friend. 'Ah've no' been masel since the caurs finished. They were sort o' ma life, ma hobby. Ye understaun?'

'A hobby. Gettin' a sore neck everyday carrying aroon a ticket machine an' a bag o' money? Then havin' tae shout at drunks an' nyaffs.'

'Och, they wurnae a bad lot really. Just liked a wee drink noo an' again.'

'So, whit are ye going tae dae noo? Ur ye goin' ontae the buses?'

'Naw, naw. Ah've heard o' umpteen conductresses who've changed tae the buses an' they've given up efter aboot a month. They were aw black an' blue wi fallin'. Ye see ye get used tae the motion o' the tram on rails o' er the years, but a bus jumps aboot aw o'er the place. Anyway, ah'm really quite sentimental aboot the caurs... in fact ah'm quite a sensitive person.'

'Sensitive! You! Ah've seen ye kick six footers aff yer tram.'

'Aye, but that wis aw in the line o' business. Ah cannae get the trams oot o' ma mind, Maisie. It's sort of... well... like a bereavement in the family. Ah still

feel the caur vibrations in ma bones. Ah just loved that
number 9 tae Auchenshuggle. Aw the folks ah met on
it. Tae tell you the truth ah feel like moving there.
Ah kinda feel that the spirit o' the caurs is still in
Auchenshuggle. In fact sumbuddy wis tellin' me that
oan a dark night a phantom number 9, ablaze wi' light,
comes oot o' nowhere and disappears intae the darkness.'

'Aggie, ye cannae really believe that. The trams are
awa. Finished. Deid. Yer hame is the Gorbals. Ye wur
born there, Aggie. Whit wid ye dae in Auchenshuggle?
Anyway, wid yer man move wi' ye tae Auchenshuggle?'

'Ma man! Tommy, och he's no' a bad soul. As lang
as there's a pub nearby Tommy wull be happy, believe
me. Anyway, if Auchenshuggle is guid enough fur Oor
Wullie in the *Sunday Post* then it's good enough fur me.'

'Aggie, don't be daft. Oor Wullie's a fictional
character.'

'Och, ah know that, but ah cannae get the place oot
ma system. It wis the end o' the line fur ma trams an'
fur me, tae. So, ah've jist made up ma mind. Ah'm
going tae flit tae Auchenshuggle.'

'But Aggie ye've goat a corporation hoose. Ye wid
need an exchange tae Auchenshuggle. Might be
difficult fae the Gorbals.'

'Maisie, yer ma best freen. The morra ah'm gonnae
go an' see the Corporation Housin' Department up at
20 Trongate. You can come wi' me if ye like.'

On the following day Aggie and Maisie found themselves in Glasgow's Corporation Housing Department
waiting area. Aggie was nervous. She had gone through
quite a few cigarettes before her name was called and
she was shown into a Housing Inspector's office.

There a shock awaited Aggie. Her heart sank.
Behind a huge desk sat Inspector Campbell, a sinister
smile on his face. The uniform and cap had gone but
in their place was a smart lounge suit.

'Good morning, Mrs MacDonald, and your friend,
too. Please sit down,' and he indicated two seats in
front of his desk. Once they were
seated he clasped his hands on the
desk. 'Now, what can I do for
you, Mrs MacDonald?'

'How on earth did you get this
job, Inspector?' asked an
incredulous Aggie.

'As I was a long time senior
employee of the City Fathers, I
have been given a position appropriate to my status,' he smirked.

'Well, Inspector... sur,' began
Aggie, 'You, better than anyone,
will understand ma request.' Aggie
stopped, then blurted out, 'Ah want
tae go an' live in Auchenshuggle.'

Campbell laughed. 'Why?'

Aggie was hesitant again. It did sound a wee bit embarrassing. 'It's because o' the trams. Ah've worked oan them fur years an' years, an' ah've been so many times at the crossover at Auchenshuggle that ah feel ah belang there. So if you could jist get me a wee hoose there ah wid be obliged. Fur auld times sake, ye could say.'

'Mrs MacDonald, on a number of occasions you almost finished my esteemed career as a Transport Inspector. I am now a Housing Inspector and I certainly do not owe you any favours. Anyway, if I remember your family circumstances correctly you must be well down our priority list.'

'Well, ah'm fed up wi' that room an' kitchen in the Gorbals. Ah don't want tae stay there. It wull soon be pulled doon an' ah'll get a new hoose in the Gorbals. So it wid be guid if sumbuddy could swap wi' me an' they would get the new Corporation hoose. So whit can ah dae tae get a hoose in Auchenshuggle?'

'Well, if you have money, and I would doubt if you have,' replied Campbell. 'then you could purchase a property. Right now there are very few Corporation houses in the Auchenshuggle area though there are plans to rectify that in the next few years. Or you could wait until you come to the top of the points system... in about a hundred years time, no doubt!'

Aggie's eyes narrowed. Her face flushed.

'Maisie, let's get oot o' here. This wee megalomaniac husnae changed. He wid gie ye the boke, so he wid. If this wis a tram, Campbell, ah wid kick yer erse aff it. In fact ah shoulda done that years ago.' And she stomped out of the office followed by Campbell's laughter.

In George Square the friends sat on a bench while Aggie calmed down. 'An' tae think ah nearly gave that wee pain a dance at the depot party, so ah did. Noo he's goat me fair bamboozled.'

'If ye ask me he's jist oot fur revenge,' observed Maisie.

'Ye'r right, Maisie. He's a conniving wee pain in the butt. Ah'll need tae take ma time an' think aboot this.'

Over the next few weeks Aggie was in despair. Her usual ebullient manner deserted her. As much as she racked her brains there seemed to be no solution to her dream move. At the same time she was aware her intake of nicotine and whisky had increased.

Then, just before New Year, an invite came in the post. Some of the ex-tram employees were planning a get-together in a city hotel. Aggie didn't hesitate. Her spirits rose. It wid be so nice tae meet up wi' aw her old pals fae the depot. A new dress was purchased plus shoes and a fresh supply of her famous red lipstick. All of a sudden she was on top of the world again.

The event was a big success in a number of ways. Aggie got slightly tipsy as she happily reminisced with her old buddies over the many incidents and characters they had come across. It was also wonderful to see her old driver, Jimmy Tamson, there too.

Towards the end of the evening, the subject of Inspector Campbell came up. All hilarity ceased. No one apparently had a good word to say about him.

'Ah wonder if he ever married,' someone had asked.

'Married, tae who? Naw, naebuddy could staun that wan,' responded another.

'Well, ah heard a wee bit o' scandal aboot him recently,' somebody piped up.

Aggie was suddenly all ears.

'Ah heard he's goat a wife an' four weans in Clarkston, but he's also goat a bit o' stuff on the side up in Maryhill.'

'Dae ye know anythin' aboot this wummin in Maryhill?' Aggie asked in a low voice.

'Aye, it's that Susie thingamajig that worked in the Coplawhill Works. Ye'll remember her. All over men like a rash, she was. An' ah heard she's noo goat a wean tae him.'

The week after New Year found a determined Aggie standing each night outside the Glasgow Housing Department offices in Trongate. She wanted to see if the Inspector would make his way to Maryhill. Did he really have a bit o' stuff there?

For a few nights she had no luck as she saw Campbell duly take a bus south of the river. It was Friday night before she saw him change his routine and go to the bus stop for Maryhill Road. When Campbell got on the bus she immediately hailed a taxi and told the driver to 'follow that bus'. 'Just like in the pictures,' she thought. Although the taxi driver gave her a puzzled look he duly trailed the bus. 'Ah jist hope he's goin' tae visit this hussy,' thought Aggie. 'Fur ah could get ma death o' cold standin' ootside that Housing Department every night.'

It wasn't long before the bus stopped on Maryhill Road and the now Housing Inspector disembarked. Aggie sat watching as he crossed the road before disappearing round a corner. She quickly paid off the taxi and trundled after him, making sure she remained

some distance behind. She was just in time to see him wave to a young woman standing at a tenement window in Firhill Street, before entering her close.

'He could be in there fur hours, or aw night, or even the weekend,' she reasoned. 'Ah'll just away hame. A've seen enough. The wee rat is definitely double-crossin' his wife an' weans.'

The following week found Aggie and Maisie back in Inspector Campbell's office.

'Ah'll say this for you, Mrs MacDonald,' he smiled. 'You are nothing if not determined.'

'Aye, ah'm determined tae get a hoose in Auchenshuggle. Jist so there's nae misunderstandin', Inspector, ah wid like wan wi' a big livin' room, a big kitchen, a bathroom an' two bedrooms.'

'In yer dreams, Mrs MacDonald.'

'Well, Inspector, funnily enough ah wis havin' a dream the other night. Ah dreamed o' this housing Inspector and this nice lookin' wee wummin in Firhill Street, up in Maryhill.'

Aggie took out a packet of fags, calmly tapped one on the packet, stuck it between her teeth and lit up. She inhaled deeply, leaving a bright red circle showing on the cigarette, before blewing the smoke towards the Inspector.

Campbell's face was red. He stood, clearly not knowing how to respond. His mouth opened but no words came out.

Aggie then went on. 'Ah'm sure, Inspector, if ye check ye'll find that ah'm noo at the tap o' that famous priority list ye mentioned. Otherwise, ma dream might jist become your nightmare, sunshine.'

Inspector Campbell seemed to compose himself. He sat down but refused to meet her glaring eyes, then cleared his throat. 'You'll, erm, get a letter in the post, Mrs MacDonald, in the next week.'

Two months later the flitting had taken place. The new flat consisted of a large living room with a photograph of the Auchenshuggle tram on the wall, a commodious kitchen, bathroom and two bedrooms, all newly decorated by Glasgow Corporation and ready for the housewarming party.

Most of the old gang from the depot came to the party at Aggie's new abode, as usual laughing and joking about the old days on the caurs. The fun went on into the small hours. Everyone agreed that it was great to meet up and they should continue to do so on a regular basis.

Just before the party broke up Jimmy Tamson rose and gave a toast. 'To the tramcar, the finest vehicle ever to grace the streets o' Glesca.' Everyone raised their glasses and cheered.

Aggie chipped in. 'Listen folks, afore youse aw go hame cummoan ben the hoose tae ma bathroom, there's somethin' ah want tae show ye.'

Everyone duly trooped through the hall wondering what was so special about Aggie's new bathroom. 'Right, aw youse. Some can staun in the bathroom wi' me an' the rest wull jist have tae peer in fae the lobby.

'Dae ye remember the fourth o' September last year? Of course ye dae, ye'll never forget it. Well, as maist o' ye wull know ah wis the conductress oan the five o'clock tram fae Anderston Cross tae Auchenshuggle. But we didnae go back tae Anderston Cross but straight tae the Depot at Dalmarnock. That wis the hale service finished. Then that auld Corporation tram wis taken wi' a lot o' ithers tae Meadowside scrapyard, set oan fire tae get rid o' the wood, and the metal sold fur scrap. But before ah left the caur that night ah took a wee souvenir...an' here it is.' And she pointed to a tram driver's mirror hung above the basin. She explained, 'Tommy noo uses it tae shave wi'.'

'So, folks, ah want tae tell ye somethin'. Whit yer lookin' at noo is me an' that auld mirror.' Suddenly Aggie had a lump in her throat, a tear rolled down a cheek. 'And we're aw that remains o'... the last tram tae Auchenshuggle.'

Big Aggie's Terminus

Aggie lived to a ripe old age in Auchenshuggle. This was remarkable in view of her continued penchant for carry-outs, cigarettes, drams and her favourite sweets, soor plooms, plus numerous packets of Spangles.

At her funeral, the crematorium was overflowing, many people standing outside, all anxious to say farewell to Glasgow's famous conductress.

A frail looking Jimmy Tamson gave a brief eulogy.

'Today we have come to say goodbye to one of the best known characters in the Glasgow Transport System, for sadly, this week, Big Aggie MacDonald died at the age of 88.

'Aggie's 40-a-day habit finally finished her off; she was run over by the number 64 bus, the Auchenshuggle tram's replacement, as she crossed the road tae buy fags.

'Aggie's dying words were reputed to be, "Ah knew these bleedin' buses wid be the death o' me."… And they were.

'Aggie and I were pally for years as we were mostly on the same shifts. In all my time as her driver, Aggie never gave me the emergency three rings on the bell for help, even though ah always told her, "Aggie, if ye want me, just ringmy-thingmy." Aggie sorted everything out by herself. It must also be said that Aggie had a warm heart, an inherent goodness, and on occasion helped out mony a poor soul.

'So, let me say this in closing: Aggie, if ye ever want me, jist ringmy-thingmy.'

Aggie's coffin, with a large number 9 printed in red, then shoogled off to the Glesca Tram Depot in the sky.

The Glesca Tram Heaven

While messin' on Google,
I typed 'Auchenshuggle',
That magical heaven o' the tram.
It's full o' auld caurs,
Wi' angelic wee roars,
An' their wings flap as they clang alang.

Whaur's Big Aggie the Clippie?
(Sae sarky an' nippy)
But naebody roon here can tell.
If in heav'n there's nae trace
O' thon wisecrackin' face,
Then ah'm certain she must be... oh well.

But she's worked to reach Heaven,
(Oan a number 11),
Yes – Aggie has made it here, too.
Wi' 'Cummonangetaff!
Gie's yer fare – no yer chaff!'
She's sortin' them aw oot in the queue!

AM

Luath Press Limited

committed to publishing well written books worth reading

LUATH PRESS takes its name from Robert Burns, whose little collie Luath (*Gael.*, swift or nimble) tripped up Jean Armour at a wedding and gave him the chance to speak to the woman who was to be his wife and the abiding love of his life. Burns called one of 'The Twa Dogs' Luath after Cuchullin's hunting dog in Ossian's *Fingal*. Luath Press was established in 1981 in the heart of Burns country, and is now based a few steps up the road from Burns' first lodgings on Edinburgh's Royal Mile.

Luath offers you distinctive writing with a hint of unexpected pleasures.

Most bookshops in the UK, the US, Canada, Australia, New Zealand and parts of Europe either carry our books in stock or can order them for you. To order direct from us, please send a £sterling cheque, postal order, international money order or your credit card details (number, address of cardholder and expiry date) to us at the address below. Please add post and packing as follows: UK – £1.00 per delivery address; overseas surface mail – £2.50 per delivery address; overseas airmail – £3.50 for the first book to each delivery address, plus £1.00 for each additional book by airmail to the same address. If your order is a gift, we will happily enclose your card or message at no extra charge.

ILLUSTRATION: IAN KELLAS

Luath Press Limited
543/2 Castlehill
The Royal Mile
Edinburgh EH1 2ND
Scotland

Telephone: 0131 225 4326 (24 hours)
Fax: 0131 225 4324
email: sales@luath.co.uk
Website: www.luath.co.uk